AFRICAN ETHNOGRAPHIC STUDIES
OF THE 20TH CENTURY

Volume 43

THE CHANGING ECONOMY OF THE
LOWER VOLTA 1954–67

THE CHANGING ECONOMY OF THE LOWER VOLTA 1954–67

A Study in the Dynanics of Rural Economic Growth

ROWENA M. LAWSON

LONDON AND NEW YORK

First published in 1972 by Oxford University Press for the International African Institute.

This edition first published in 2018
by Routledge
2 Park Square, Milton Park, Abingdon, Oxon OX14 4RN

and by Routledge
711 Third Avenue, New York, NY 10017

Routledge is an imprint of the Taylor & Francis Group, an informa business

© 1972 International African Institute

All rights reserved. No part of this book may be reprinted or reproduced or utilised in any form or by any electronic, mechanical, or other means, now known or hereafter invented, including photocopying and recording, or in any information storage or retrieval system, without permission in writing from the publishers.

Trademark notice: Product or corporate names may be trademarks or registered trademarks, and are used only for identification and explanation without intent to infringe.

British Library Cataloguing in Publication Data
A catalogue record for this book is available from the British Library

ISBN: 978-0-8153-8713-8 (Set)
ISBN: 978-0-429-48813-9 (Set) (ebk)
ISBN: 978-1-138-59111-0 (Volume 43) (hbk)
ISBN: 978-0-429-49063-7 (Volume 43) (ebk)

Publisher's Note
The publisher has gone to great lengths to ensure the quality of this reprint but points out that some imperfections in the original copies may be apparent.

Disclaimer
The publisher has made every effort to trace copyright holders and would welcome correspondence from those they have been unable to trace.

The Changing Economy of the Lower Volta 1954-67

A study in the Dynamics of Rural Economic Growth

ROWENA M. LAWSON

Senior Research Fellow, University of Leeds
Formerly Senior Lecturer, University of Ghana

Based on research undertaken under the auspices of the Volta Basin Research Project, University of Ghana

Published for the
INTERNATIONAL AFRICAN INSTITUTE
by
OXFORD UNIVERSITY PRESS
LONDON NEW YORK TORONTO
1972

Oxford University Press, Ely House, London W. 1

GLASGOW NEW YORK TORONTO MELBOURNE WELLINGTON
CAPE TOWN SALISBURY IBADAN NAIROBI DAR ES SALAAM LUSAKA ADDIS ABABA
BOMBAY CALCUTTA MADRAS KARACHI LAHORE DACCA
KUALA LUMPUR SINGAPORE HONG KONG TOKYO

ISBN 0 19 724188 3

© International African Institute 1972

Typeset by H. Charlesworth & Co. Ltd., Huddersfield.
Printed in Great Britain by
Redwood Press Ltd. Trowbridge, Wiltshire

TO PENNY AND LAWRENCE

Contents

PREFACE

PART I

1. Introduction	1
2. Methodology	6

PART II The Empirical Study

1. General Features of the Economy	12
2. Agriculture	30
3. Volta Fisheries	45
4. The Clam Industry	51
5. Cattle	57
6. Changes in Trading Activities in the Lower Volta, 1954–64	61
7. Changes in Income and Wealth, 1954–64	79

PART III

Economic Processes of Change	91
Bibliography	117
Index	121

TABLES
page

1. Population of twelve largest villages in Tongu Local Council District in Lower Volta — 17
2. Places of centrality — 19
3. Population of places of centrality giving birthplace and employment in 1960 — 21
4. Occupational structure of Tongu District and Battor (Main occupations only), as percentage of total occupation — 24
5. Employment in agriculture, 1954 and 1964 — 36
6. End use of agricultural output in 1954 and 1964 — 36
7. Comparative data on agriculture over 1310 acres in the vicinity of Battor, 1954 and 1964 — 37
8. Non-labour inputs into agriculture as a percentage of total population — 41
9. Comparisons of real earnings from agriculture, 1954 and 1964, in Battor — 42
10. The distribution of capital and earnings between 36 fishermen in 1954 and 50 fishermen in 1964 — 46
11. Distribution of earning from fishing in 1954 (between 36 men) and 1964 (between 50 men) — 49
12. Distribution of labour input into fishing in 1964 — 50
13. Differences in clam production, 1954–1964 — 54
14. Stocks, turnover and profits of stores in Battor in 1954 — 65
15. Comparative size of Aveyime market in 1954 and 1964 — 67
16. Goods for sale in Aveyime market, 1954 and 1964 — 68
17. Market trade in Adidome and Sogakope, 1964, main items of produce only — 72
18. Turnover of goods in stores in Battor in 1954 and 1964 as percentage of total turnover — 73
19. Stocks, turnover and profits of stores in Battor, 1964 — 74
20. Structure of aggregate income for Battor, including value of subsistence production — 81
21. Monthly household income levels in Battor, 1954 and 1964, in £'s sterling at current prices — 82

22.	Aggregate ownership of goods and property in Battor, 1954 and 1967 at 1966 prices in Ghana £'s	83
23.	Numbers and values of house buildings in Battor, 1954 and 1967 at 1967 prices in £'s sterling	84
24.	Main sources of earnings of funds used for investment in house-building in Battor and Adidome between 1964 and 1967	85
25.	Distribution of total value of assets of households taking all households in Battor in 1954 and 1967	86
26.	Number of items of specific durable household goods owned in Battor in 1954 and 1967	86

MAP

Lower reaches of Volta River, Akusu-Ada, before 1964   xiv

Preface

The field work for this study was mainly undertaken in the Lower Volta, Ghana, first in 1954 and later over the period 1964–67. The work of collecting data for the latter period was financed by the Rockefeller Foundation and the main purpose was to make a study of rural economic growth over a ten year period, 1954–64, using as benchmark data, material collected by the author in 1954 in the course of a study of the economy of the Lower Volta undertaken for the Volta River Project Preparatory Commission. This Commission was appointed by the British Government in 1952 to undertake preparatory work for the proposal to exploit local bauxite deposits and to develop large scale aluminium production using hydroelectric power from the proposed Volta dam. This scheme, which would have involved Canadian and British aluminium producers and the British and Gold Coast Governments, was finally abandoned in 1956.

I would like to thank Sir Robert Jackson who was Director of the V.R.P.P.C., for his permission to use data collected whilst I was employed by the Commission. I would also like to thank the Rockefeller Foundation for financial support for the field work undertaken since 1964. The Food Research Institute, Stanford University generously gave facilities for the analysis and writing up of the data and the author would like especially to thank all those members of the Institute who gave valuable criticism and help during her employment as Associate Professor at Stanford, in particular Dr W. O. Jones, Dr Carl Eicher and Dr John Jamison.

Some aspects of this study were introduced in the discussions at the International African Seminar on The Development of Indigenous Trade and Markets in West

PREFACE

Africa, held under the auspices of the International African Institute at Fourah Bay College, Sierra Leone, in December 1969. Thanks are due to the Institute for undertaking its publication.

The University of Leeds has also assisted towards the publication of this monograph and their generosity is acknowledged. Thanks must also go the Volta Basin Research Project, University of Ghana, under whose aegis this work was carried out and which also gave some financial help, and to Walter Pople, Zoology Department, for his unstinting help in innumerable ways in the field.

This study would not have been possible without the assistance of a large number of recorders and research assistants in the field. They are too many to mention by name but I would like to thank them all for their patience and persistence in working under difficult physical conditions in an area which, at the time, was fairly remote.

Lastly, I would like to thank the people of Battor, the chief and elders and the local council officers who suffered our observations and enquiries for so long.

Rowena M. Lawson

University of Leeds
January 1971

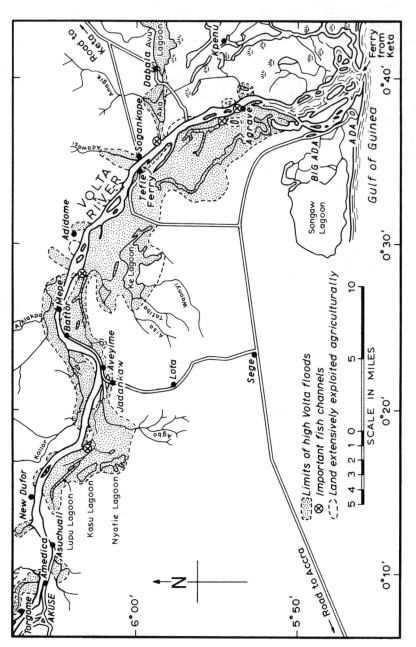

LOWER REACHES OF VOLTA RIVER, AKUSE – ADA, BEFORE 1964.

PART I

1 Introduction

The purpose of this study is to examine the process of growth of a rural economy in Ghana over a period of fourteen years from 1954–67 based on an empirical study. During these years the economy under observation moved from the static traditional Schultzian-type equilibrium (Schultz, 1964, chapters 1 and 2), which had been confined by a closely knit socio-economic matrix, into a transitory phase of economic growth in which earlier constraints were broken down to make way for a more sensitive response to economic opportunity. It cannot be said however that by 1967 self-sustaining economic growth had been achieved. This study is an attempt to assess the factors which disturbed the static equilibrium of this rural economy and enabled it to move to a higher level of economic activity.

Field data were obtained by a combination of regular statistical recording and data collection, and also by close observations made during periods of residence in the village of Battor between 1954 and 1967. The amount of quantitative data collected will be obvious from the empirical data presented here, but it is most important to stress that the understanding and interpretation of this material would not have been possible without close observations of the socio-cultural changes which were occurring simultaneously over this period. This study represents the first examination of the interaction of socio-economic variables at a micro level over a significant period of economic change.

The rural economy which forms the subject of this study is the riparian community of the Lower Volta which had a population of some 54,000 in 1954 which formed a homogeneous society by tribe (Ewe), by sources of income and by social institutions. In general, the social and economic characteristics of this area are probably typical of much of the present rural economy of Ghana. Its proximity to the river however has provided a source of income from fishing which exists only in other riparian or coastal areas of Ghana but this had not led to a higher level of income or wealth than is found elsewhere. The amount of economic change which took place over the period discussed here is probably very similar to that occurring simultaneously in other rural areas in Ghana. This study aims to distinguish the major socio-economic preconditions for this increase in economic activity. In the light of empirical observations an examination is made of some of the accepted concepts of development of rural economies which are, like this, undergoing a very early process of growth.

The riparian people of the Lower Volta are traditionally farmers and fishermen. Until the completion of the Volta dam in 1963 the economy of the riparian communities was very dependent on the annual floods of the river which occurred between July and September. These left behind valuable irrigated farm land and a large number of ponds and creeks which supported a prolific fishery. After 1963 the annual floods ceased, the river began to maintain a steady annual flow and the riparian communities were denied the economic advantages of natural irrigation and water supplies for inland fisheries. In anticipation of a loss of income from these sources, the Volta River Project Preparatory Commission, which had been established by the British Government in 1953 to investigate the feasibility of the construction of a dam on the River Volta, instituted a study to ascertain to what extent the riparian economy lying below the dam site depended on the annual flooding of the river (Volta River Project, 1956). This study provides the bench mark data used here.

The study made of the riparian communities of the Lower Volta resulted in the recommendation that some £500,000 should be set aside to mitigate the effects which would follow the construction of the dam. £350,000 of this would be for compensation for the loss of fisheries in creeks and ponds. Agricultural production would also decline owing to

INTRODUCTION 3

decrease in yields of crops hitherto grown on naturally irrigated land but, rather than pay compensation for this loss, the VRPPC recommended that the Government should introduce agricultural improvements (Volta River Project 1956, p. 59, paras. 373–82).

In the area around Battor which was studied in 1954 (and later in 1964–67) it was found that some 25% of direct aggregate income of the community was derived from the river and its annual floods. This figure however represents only the value of agriculture and fisheries which would be lost by the cessation of annual floods. If linkage and multiplier effects had been taken into account the importance of the floods to the economy of the Lower Volta would have been much higher than this. When the Volta dam was eventually completed in 1963–4, the economy of Ghana had undergone many changes, and there was no provision in the plans of Volta River Authority, which administered the Volta scheme, for paying compensation to those riparian communities living downstream. The long term effects of the construction of the dam on the economy downstream depends on both the response of the riparian communities to economic change and also to government decisions about investment in new inputs especially in social overheads, infrastructure and agricultural improvements. In the short period to date however, despite the lack of cash compensation, the people living downstream have benefited from the construction of the dam, especially owing to the emergence of a valuable lake fishery.

When this developed after 1964 it was immediately exploited by many people from the riparian communities of the Lower Volta who moved temporarily upstream for fishing. Later they returned to their home communities downstream with an unprecedented level of earnings. These were largely used on a spending spree, especially in the improvement and construction of houses.

On the basis of quantitative measures of the standard of living, wealth and ownership of goods, it would appear that the communities underwent a sudden rapid rate of economic growth. However a significant finding of this study is that the socio-economic preconditions for this display of economic gain had been building up over a period, since the bench mark study of 1954 had shown the economy to be static. These preconditions mainly involved a breakdown of the established socio-cultural constraints imposed by the traditional society. Since 1954 many social, economic and political forces of change had been introduced from exogenous sources. These had operated in a way which distrubed the previous static equilibrium. For example the political power of the chief and the institutions surrounding him were seriously eroded by the introduction of party politics to Ghana and later, after Independence in 1957, by the emergence of a one party state and the infiltration of a party organisation into rural life. Newcomers to the rural economy, mainly wage and salary earners who were employed in the new schools and hospitals and on construction and road building brought new demands for foodstuffs, exhibited a variety of new imported goods and brought new ways of living to the community. Improvements in roads and markets gave greater contact with other areas and subjected the rural economy to influences of urban life.

Such influences gradually began to erode the hitherto unquestioning acceptance of traditional institutions and the stability and security they offered. As these began to diminish, the people were forced to find new institutions to suit the changing socio-economic environment.

This study shows that perhaps the most important need of the individual in an environment which is undergoing economic change is for security. In a period of growing per capita incomes those funds earned as surplus to the culturally determined level of subsistence are set aside for the future in a conscious preference for future goods over present goods. However few suitable investment opportunities for surplus funds exist which have the conditions required by the rural saver. There are few banks or post offices and these are in many cases not trusted for their secrecy. He cannot invest in agricultural innovation since this is unknown to him. This is partly a failure of extension services but also a failure to provide agricultural improvements which are feasable within the limits set by the availability of land, labour and farm management.

Once the customary and socially-acceptable improvements have been made to family houses, the rural saver in this society uses his surplus funds as a cash hoard, or as an investment in cattle or on educational expenses. These two latter appear to be the best investment opportunities open to him within his own cultural environment. Other investments, e.g. in lorry transport or in building houses for letting would involve him in a new environment, probably an urban one.

In spite of the appearance of a static traditional economy which persisted for many years, this rural community was not one which was constrained by limited aspirations or by the complacent achievement of target incomes. It was a society which, throughout a period of income growth, had been surreptitiously saving for the future in a search for security to replace the security previously given by institutions of the traditional culture which had been gradually eroded by economic growth. This search for security takes precedence over the demand for a rise in the standard of living. The popular model of a consumer-oriented economy in which the individual is spurred to greater effort by the consumer goods of a western shop window does not apply to a rural economy at the stage of growth described here. It may apply to a higher level of development or to an urban economy, but initially, as a static gives way to a growing economy, the overriding need is for security. This is reflected not only in the ways in which the individual uses his surplus funds but also in the way in which he uses his so-called 'leisure' and in his attitudes to religion and to his family.

2 Methodology

The 1954 study consisted partly of a micro-study of a typical riparian community with a population of some 1,050 persons and a less detailed study of the wider riparian areas of the Lower Volta. The area chosen for detailed study surrounded the village of Battor, in the Tongu District, which had a 1954 resident population of 566, and eleven small villages and hamlets nearby which had a total population of 491. In 1954 there were 70 such small villages and hamlets within 10 miles of Battor which had some cultural affinity to Battor based on extended family relationships and which were known as 'Battor hamlets'. The economic recording in Battor consisted of first, data on all sources of income, some of which was based on daily recordings of farming and fishing earnings at source so that the value of production for both subsistence and the market was obtained. Secondly, data on earnings were cross checked by daily observation and weighing of farm off-take, of fish landed and of clams which were taken from the river by women divers. Measurement of all lands under cultivation were made according to crops grown and potential production was valued on the basis of crop price estimates.

Over a five month period, daily household expenditure records were taken in a 5% sample of households. Expenditure data were cross checked by recording purchases in the market and stores. Monthly accounting and stock taking procedures were instituted in all the stores and this yielded accurate data on turnover, profits and prices. Records of transactions in the Battor village market yielded similar information. Quantitative recording in the market at Aveyime, some three miles from Battor, which was held twice weekly, of the volume of trade, number of traders, price sources of goods in the market gave material which provided cross checks to the level of earnings from sales of produce. All goods entering Battor were recorded over a five month period by daily road and riverside checks. Studies of the food consumption in a sample of households based on daily recordings of weight of food consumed over a period of three months enabled data on nutritional status to be compiled and also provided some cross check to the amount of production used for home consumption.

In assessing the per capita earnings in Battor the methodology of national accounting procedures used in Ghana (Walters, 1962) was adapted to the data obtained. Though direct questions on earnings were asked, answers were found to be very unreliable except from wage and salary earners. Most people are probably reluctant to divulge information on income but in many cases in Battor, individuals did not know what their earnings were when asked to give them in terms of monthly or annual earnings, and it was only by relating earnings to sources of income that any realistic figure could be arrived at. The accounting system adopted is outlined below.

INCOME	(cash earnings plus production for subsistence)	=
PRODUCTION	(value of farm and fish production plus value of earnings of salaried and self employed persons)	=
EXPENDITURE AND SAVINGS	(Aggregated household expenditure plus savings)	

Income and production data were recorded at source. Expenditure data were recorded at point of sale and cross checked by household expenditure data. The sources of data collection are listed.

INCOME AND PRODUCTION RECORDED AT SOURCE

1. Food Farming. Daily records.
2. Clam Fishing. Daily records.
3. Creek and River Fishing. Daily records.

4. Trading and Store-keeping. Daily and monthly records.
5. Others, including skilled labour and crafts, unskilled labour, and all salaried employments. Records taken at source of employment.

EXPENDITURE RECORDED AT POINT OF SALE

i *Expenditure incurred in Battor.*
(a) Local foods—checked by market trader's sales.
(b) Imported foods—checked by storekeeper's sales.
(c) Local drink and imported drink—checked with (a) and (b) above.

ii *Expenditure incurred out of Battor.*
Checked by recording all imports of goods by river and road into Battor.

The only item on which satisfactory field data could not be obtained relates to certain capital transactions, specifically to savings which were treated as a residual to income and expenditure. Loans and debts were more easy to identify and a seasonal movement in small capital transactions was observed. Just before the commencement of the fishing season it was often necessary for fishermen to borrow money to renew and repair equipment. Many households also became very short of funds just before the first harvest. A considerable amount of small short-term capital transactions took place to cover these situations but such lending was mostly between friends or relatives and bore no interest payment and few debts remained outstanding for very long. Larger capital transactions existed mostly between owners of creeks or land and money lenders, and usually involved the mortgage of property or real estate. Such transactions were often public knowledge. Large debts were rarely encountered except for the payment of litigation concerning ownership of land and creeks, such as arose from a small number of family and clan feuds which had been carried on for generations. Again these were usually known to the community.

Savings took two major forms, first cash which was usually hoarded seasonally in or near the house and which was used to supply the household needs for cash during the year and secondly, savings invested, usually for a longer period, in a

METHODOLOGY 9

hoard, mostly by the purchase of cattle and less frequently, by the purchase of gold. These methods of saving can be rationalised in the context of the rural economy. There were no institutional means of saving in the aaea, there was no bank or post office. For a number of reasons, for example the fear of theft or of having excessive demands made from the extended family, individuals preferred to keep their savings secret, even from spouses. The practice of purchasing cattle, which is described in detail later, is considered here to perform some of the functions of a savings bank.

In addition to the micro-study in Battor, wider surveys over the entire stretch of the river between Amedica and Tefle were made. This stretch which covers some 32 miles is the most valuable part of the Lower Volta lying some 22 miles from the mouth of the river at Ada. The whole of this area was affected by annual river floods and the most important sources of income were similar to those in Battor, namely fishing, farming and diving for clams. Throughout this stretch of the river bi-monthly counts were made of all clam divers, detailed studies of the economics of clam diving and clam trading were made in the Akuse area (Lawson, 1963). All creeks and water courses, totalling 394 were visited by officers of the VRPPC and the value of fish yields estimated. All lands under crops were also visited by the VRPPC and acreages under each crop was measured. Data from these wider areas enabled an assessment of the economy of the entire riparian community to be made.

By 1964 however, the whole riparian economy had moved to a higher level of activity in which there was a greater movement of goods and people, a higher level of production, more diversified sources of income and a more advanced infrastructure. These made it impossible to record in detail with the staff available, data from the wider area. In particular no detailed records were taken of land under different types of crop along the entire riparian area and it was not possible to study fish production in creeks except those in the vicinity of Battor which were fished by Battor men. However a full study of clam production was made in the entire Lower Volta, based on bi-monthly journeys up and down the river between Tefle and Akuse. Certain other studies however were made in 1964 which were not made in 1954, notably a study of cattle farming on the eastern bank of the river and a study of labour input into farming (Lawson, 1967a, 1968a). Apart from these exceptions, data were collected in 1964 from all sources used in the 1954 study.

After the completion of the detailed study in 1964 the area was visited regularly until 1967 and certain socio-economic changes were observed closely and surveys over a wider area in the Lower Volta were made. These included studies of the four major markets at Adidome, Akuse, Aveyime and Sogakope in which regular market recordings of produce for sale were made, studies of cattle farming on the east side of the river and observation on house building and business enterprises were made in the main large villages, described later as 'places of centrality' (Lawson, 1970). In addition, records of house building were made in Battor throughout 1964–67 which included estimating the costs of each building on the basis of the cost of input used.

Another aspect of research was the study of diets. For one month in 1954 and 1964 the diets of five comparable households were recorded by daily weighing the food consumed by each household. Diets were subsequently analysed and a considerable improvement in the standard of nutrition was found in 1964 over the 1954 level both in respect of protein and calorie content. These studies (Lawson, 1957, 1967b) do not form an integral part of the work discussed here but the findings support the evidence of rising rural living standards.

In 1954 detailed daily recordings were taken over a five-month period, coinciding with the period of greatest economic activity, but other less detailed data were collected throughout the year by the staff of the Volta River Project Preparatory Commission. For the study of Battor and its vicinity, and the agricultural, fisheries and marketing data described here, a team of field assistants was formed. This consisted of two Statistical Assistants, seconded from the Central Bureau of Statistics, a Fisheries Assistant and his assistant, seconded from the government Fisheries Department, and an Agricultural Assistant and his assistant, seconded from the government Department of Agriculture. Four locally recruited field recorders were employed as required.

In 1964—67 the field team was recruited from diverse sources. Fortunately the author was able to recruit the same person to undertake the field work concerned with fisheries as in 1954. The agricultural work was undertaken by an ex-government Agricultural Officer. Two Research Assistants were recruited from the army and the Forestry Department and these two carried out the day to day research and supervision of field recorders in Battor and its vicinity and made regular recordings of market data. During the easter vacation 1964, eight students of the School of Administration, University of Ghana, undertook the basic mapping and enumeration of households in Battor and counted livestock and canoes owned by villagers. As in 1954, a number of local people were recruited as part-time field recorders and assistants. Some of these had also been employed in the 1954 study.

Intensive research and supervision in 1954 and 1964 was undertaken by the author during periods of residence in Battor, and at other times at week-ends.

PART II

THE EMPIRICAL STUDY

1 General Features of the Economy

i. *Sociology*

The riparian communities of the Lower Volta in 1954 were economically static, geographically remote and, in some areas, only on the fringe of a cash economy. Depopulation of the area had been gradually taking place over generations by the migration of Tongu fishermen to places on the upper stretches of the river. Levels of income and ownership and wealth were below average for the country but probably similar to much of rural Ghana outside the cocoa belt. The traditional social structure discouraged great inequalities in income and wealth. Social life was constrained in a matrix of socio-cultural mores in which pagan religion thrived. Nearly all except the salary earners and school children were illiterate. The political structure based on the traditional status of the chief and a few dominant clans gave little opportunity for the emergence of new leaders.

There appeared to be no opportunity for the development from within this framework of an entrepreneurial or innovating farming class which would break through this equilibrium to provide some basis for economic growth. There was a high subsistence sector, which, though as low as 30% in the larger villages such as Battor, where there were a few opportunities for wage employment, was as high as 70% in smaller villages and hamlets. A great amount of time was spent on apparently non-productive functions, e.g. funerals, visiting friends and litigation. Levels of consumption were culturally determined and low by national standards and windfalls were spent in acceptable prestige expenditure, e.g. funerals, festivities, and, amongst the wealthier land owning families, litigation. Little diversity in sources of income occurred; nearly all were engaged in primary industry in farming and fishing. The more diverse employment structure which existed in Battor was probably typical of only some 8–9 villages in the entire riparian area and these together had an aggregate population of less than 10% of the total.

Prior to the construction of the dam the most economically valuable stretch of the whole of the Volta river was that which lay between Tefle and Amedica where fishing and agriculture provided most income.

A major reason for the static nature of the economy in 1954 was the low level of communications. The riparian population living between Tefle and Amedica depended almost entirely on canoe transport on the river. The only motor vessel on the river in 1954 was the United Africa Company's launch which plied up and down stream between Ada and Amedica on alternate days. A rough eleven mile track across the Accra plains connected Aveyime on the river, some 15 miles downstream from Amedica, with Sege on the main Accra-Tefle road. This track was extended later to Battor and Mepe but was rarely plied with lorries and when the survey commenced in 1954 the middle of the road was deeply grass covered and motorable only during the dry season. After 1954 the Public Works Department improved part of the road in order to obtain access to deposits of stone which existed some 4 miles from Aveyime, but the road beyond Aveyime into Battor which was maintained by the Tongu District Council was intersected by a number of heavy swamp regions which flooded annually. The only other motorable track in the district was between Sogakope and Adidome on the east bank but this too was subject to seasonal inundation from floods and heavy rain.

The poor state of communications was reflected in a low level of trade and market activity. The most important markets were at Akuse, adjacent to the river port of Amedica, and at Tefle where a small market supplied the ferry traffic. Other markets existed at Adidome and Aveyime. The former was primarily used as a point of transit for onions and fish from the Keta district on the coast to Akuse upstream which served as a distribution point for the cocoa growing region to north and west. Some rice and maize grown in the hinterland of Adidome also passed through this market, mainly en route for Accra. Aveyime had no appreciable transit trade at this time, though it served as a collecting centre for clams, groundnuts, sweet potato and maize grown in the vicinity and in areas across the river for forward despatch mainly to Accra, Akuse and Koforidua. The volume of trade in Aveyime was limited by its seasonal inaccessibility by road.

The limited contact with other markets was reflected in the low level of trade in and consumption of imported goods. Only the largest villages had any stores which sold imported goods. Battor had four such stores at the beginning of 1954. Aveyime had only three, Tefle had two. Adidome had two comparatively large stores owned by expatriate trading companies and five small African-owned stores. Akuse had a more thriving trade in imported goods, having two expatriate-owned stores, four African-owned stores and a market trade in imported goods. The turnover of the small African-owned stores was in the region of £240 to £400 per annum, probably over half of this being accounted for by drinks, cigarettes and tobacco.

There are no statistics on literacy in the area but the 1960 Population Census revealed that 56% of the males and 80% of the females in the rural section of the Volta Region had never been to school (Population Census of Ghana, 1960, vol. 2, p. xvii). This may be taken as a fair indication of the level of illiteracy in the Tongu Local Council district. In 1954 most of the larger villages had one Primary School, and there were three Middle Schools in the district, supported by the Roman Catholic and Presbyterian Churches. Compulsory primary education was not introduced until 1960 and by 1967 was still inadequate.

Health in the district is affected by the presence of water-borne diseases in the river and creeks. Malaria and bilharzia are very common. Two surveys made by Medical Field Units in 1954—5 in Central Tongu showed a high incidence of certain diseases, e.g. malaria 30%, bilharzia 23%, onchocerciasis (which produces river blindness) 11%. Just outside the geographical limits of this study however the incidence of onchocerciasis was reported to be 68% of total population and 92% of adult males (Volta River Project, 1956. Appendix vii, para. 71, Appendix viii, para 45).

In 1954, the general status of nutrition in the area appeared to be just adequate though physical effort and productivity were obviously affected by the prevalence of disease. Cassava provided the main staple and there were fair quantities of groundnuts, peppers, palm oil and some vegetables to supply vitamins whilst fresh or dried fish and clams provided protein, but diets varied seasonally with the availability of seasonal foods, especially protein foods.

Houses were constructed mostly of mud and thatch using household labour and most were less than £20 in value. Very few houses were made of more durable materials. Cement was used in a few cases in the construction of floors and, in the larger villages, possibly one quarter to one half of the houses had some iron roofing. Many households maintained more than one dwelling in the area. People living in hamlets in the area were often members of an extended family with rights to use the family house in the large village where the clan originated. It is customary for a successful male member of the household to build a house in his native village, or to improve on the existing family house and this has been the traditional manner of exhibiting status and achievement for generations.

Kinship ties with those who have left the area to live elsewhere are strong in spite of the general depopulation. This is evidenced by three phenomena, first there is an annual influx in November and December of members of a clan who have been temporary migrants, most of whom return from fishing upstream. Secondly importance is placed on burial of the dead in the home village of the clan, bodies being brought sometimes 100 miles for burial. Thirdly there is emphasis on the maintenance of family houses and a great deal of expenditure continues to be made on family houses which have no economic value for renting. Pagan religion continues to have an important role in the community in spite of the increasing activity of Christian religions (Population Census of Ghana, 1960, Special Report E. pp. xxi–xxii). Some decrease in the strength of kinship ties was evident by 1964.

ii. *Population changes between 1954—67*

The riparian communities of the Lower Volta totalled 54,000 people in 1954. They formed part of the wider Tongu Local Council District which, according to the Censuses, had a population of 86,056 in 1960 and 103,000 in 1948. It is somewhat difficult to extract complete comparative data from the Censuses of 1948 and 1960 since the enumeration districts were different in each of them and a number of villages were named or grouped differently. It has, however, been possible to extract comparative data on the occupations and populations of the twelve largest villages of this District and this is shown in Table 1. Other comparative data were obtained by examining Census sheets at source. The results of these findings and also those based on observations made in the empirical studies of 1954 and 1964—67 enabled certain generalisations on population change to be made.

The two most impotant population changes which have taken place since 1954 are the emergence of a few places of centrality and an overall decline in population in the area. A place of centrality is defined by Grove and Huszar (1964) on the basis of a ranking determined by the presence of various urban-type institutions, such as local government offices, police posts, post offices, stores, markets, churches, hospitals, etc.

The emergence of places of centrality can be considered as a function of a number of inputs. Most important of these in this area has been the investment of government in establishing local government offices and administrative centres since the independence of Ghana in 1957. This has led not only to an increase in building construction, but also to a growth of wage employments. Local government growth has been supported in most places by investment in roads. Another important government-financed input has been investment in schools, clinics, and hospitals. In some areas, notably in Aveyime and Adidome, government Agricultural Stations have been established to carry out experimental work involving irrigation, rice, sugar and vegetable farming.

In addition to government investment in the area there has been some social service investment from Christian Missions, notably in Battor, where the Roman Catholic Mission con-

GENERAL FEATURES OF THE ECONOMY 17

TABLE I

Population of twelve largest villages in Tongu
Loval Council District in Lower Volta
(Source, 1948 and 1960 Censuses)

Village	Population 1948*	Population 1960*	Birthplace of 1960 Population (from 1960 census**)		
			This Locality	Another Locality, same region	Elsewhere
Adutor	2,854	2,144	1,917	168	59
Adidome	874	1,950	698	836	416
Sogakope	365	1,790	468	810	512
Mepe	1,258	1,652	1,473	124	55
Sokpor	290	1,276	1,141	86	49
Tefle	403	1,469	656	462	351
Agbakorpe	1,182	1,161	1,024	122	15
Volo	763	1,122	786	235	101
Bakpa	618	735	708	26	1
Vume	598	679	587	75	17
Battor	520	661	470	140	51
Sasekpre	780	623	542	70	11
Total	10,539	15,262	10,470	3,154	1,638
Population of other villages and hamlets in Tongu L.C.	92,533	70,794			
Total population of Tongu L.C.	103,072	86,056			

* Figures have been obtained by comparing populations of each individual village and hamlet, since these were grouped differently in the Census of 1948 and 1960.

** No details are available from 1948 Census.

structed a hospital, clinic and nurses training school and a Middle School, and at Adidome where the Presbyterian Mission was equally active.

Economic activity which followed these inputs led to pronounced spatial movements of population, the most obvious being the movement from the highly dispersed rural pattern of 1954 to a more concentrated one. This is obvious from the statistics of the two Population Censuses 1948 and 1960 and the continuing process of increasing intensity of population was observed throughout this study. Less obvious however, but greater in size, has been the continued overall depopulation of the area and this followed the trend observed in 1954. Statistical data for the whole area are obtainable only from the Population Censuses of 1948 and 1960 though information on the places of centrality named here were obtained from field data during the course of this study.

In 1948 there were only nine villages with a population of over 500, compared with twenty-one villages in 1960. In 1948 there were only three villages with a population over 1,000; by 1960 there were eight over this size. The growth of the larger villages had been partly due to an inflow of people from dispersed communities and partly to an increase in the number of people coming from another population region (as defined by the 1960 census). This latter movement was particularly associated with the growth in wage employments in rural areas, following investments described above.

The twelve largest villages in the Tongu Local Council district had together a population which increased from 10,000 to 15,000 over the period between the Census Years (See Table 1). Though this is however only some 1,000 above a natural increase of 2.6% per annum, the 1960 Census revealed that some 3,154, i.e. some 20% of the population of the 12 largest villages had been born in another locality in the same region. Thus, it is likely that most of the increase in population is attributable to those born in hamlets and smaller villages who had since moved to larger villages.

The Censuses revealed a decrease in population living in hamlets and small villages especially those which lie away from the main transport links of road and river, many of which are now derelict.

The most significant population change however has been the emergence of four places of centrality as defined by Grove and Huszar, given in Table 2 below. These are Sogakope, Adidome, Tefle and Battor and though these were still classified in the 1960 Census as villages they have important economic functions which are generally associated with urban centres and the description 'large village' does not, in the context of a dispersed rural population, adequately describe their importance. Grove and Huszar recognised such villages as central places, developing a ranking of the centrality of such a place as a function of the variety and level of services it has to offer, the most important being administration, communications, social services. There are, on the indices given by Grove and Huszar, 35 places of centrality in the Volta Region; Ho, the regional administration centre, has 31 points of centrality and scores the highest. The four villages on the Lower Volta have the following scores:—

TABLE 2

Places of centrality

	Rank out of 35 places of centrality in the Volta Region	Score in terms of centrality functions	% of non agricultural employment
Sogakope	8	15	73
Adidome	14	8	76
Tefle	15	8	67
Battor	21	5	43

The high level of wage employment in the places of centrality is reflected in the low level of agricultural employment as a proportion to total employment. In the riparian area outside these places of centrality, agriculture (which includes fishing) is the only employment for a large proportion of the population, though some women undertake trading activities. Three of the places listed in Table 2 are also those which have experienced the greatest rate of population growth (see Tables 1 and 3). These are Sogakope, Adidome and Tefle which have increased fivefold, twofold and threefold respectively. (Sokpor, listed as the other village with high rate of growth in Table 1 in fact includes a number of dispersed villages and cannot be considered as a place of centrality.) Battor, the fourth village listed as a place of centrality has a large fluctuating population since it contains many 'family houses' of Tongu who live for most of the year in other places. This may account for its relatively low recorded population. At certain periods the population of this village may be twice as high as the figures given in the Censuses. Tefle and Sogakope are both adjacent to the ferry, and their growth can be associated with the increased traffic across the river since 1948. The growth of Adidome, now a very important collecting centre on the east bank of the river for goods passing between the hinterland and destinations on the E.–W. road, is associated with the improvement of the road from Sogakope northwards to Adidome.

Both Sogakope and Adidome have developed certain urban features since 1954 but are not officially classified as towns, since the 1960 census specifies a minimum size of 5,000 for this classification. Adidome, has in fact, increased in size since 1960 and now has many urban characteristics. Over one half of the buildings in 1964–5 were constructed of cement as distinct from mud and thatch. There is a large hospital, twenty five stores and altogether 93 separate business organizations, half of which commenced operations since 1958. Most of the new businesses including 12 transport undertakings, 10 tailors, 8 bakers, are owned and operated by 'strangers' to Adidome (i.e. not born in Adidome), nearly all of them from tribes in the East and Volta Regions. Sogakope too has developed many urban characteristics in recent years. Together Adidome, Sogakope and Tefle derived 25% of their 1960 population from outside the Volta Region.

Much of the development of these four villages has taken place since 1957 when Ghana became independent. The main motivators of growth have arisen from sources outside the indigenous rural economy, mainly from government investment. More important than the level of investment however is the value of regular flows of income from external sources which is paid to salary and wage earners employed in local and central administrative services.

Direct government investment in infrastructure has not

been very great. For instance, in the Battor–Aveyime area, the road for Sege to Aveyime cost some £50,000 and the market at Aveyime a further £5,000. Investment by the Missions is more difficult to assess since there was an input of voluntary work. Investments from external sources have had considerable multiplier effects on the rural economy. For instance, wage employments arising from government infrastructure and social service investments have increased. This has been most pronounced in Sogakope, Adidome and Tefle where, according to the 1960 Census, non-agricultural employments were some 75% of total. In Battor where detailed records were taken of occupations and earnings in 1954, payments to wage and salary earners doubled between 1954 and 1964 and provided 25% of aggregate village income.

There appears to be some correlation between the numbers of persons employed in non-agricultural employments and the numbers of persons living in the place of centrality who were not born there. This is borne out by the data given in Table 3.

TABLE 3
Population of places of centrality giving birthplace and employment in 1960 *

	Census 1948	Census 1960	This Locality	Another Locality	Elsewhere	In Agric.	Other
Sogakope	365	1,790	468	810	512	241	893
Adidome	874	1,950	698	836	416	239	987
Tefle	403	1,469	656	462	351	247	744
Battor	520	661	470	140	51	194	240
		5,870	2,292	2,248	1,330	921	2,864

(Birthplace columns: This Locality, Another Locality, Elsewhere; Employment 1960: In Agric., Other)

* Source: 1960 Census of Population

In the places of centrality given above, about one fifth of the population originates from another locality in the same region whilst nearly one quarter comes from elsewhere. The total of those born outside the locality (2,578) is strikingly similar to the numbers employed in occupations other than agriculture (which includes forestry, hunting and fishing) totalling 2,864. In Battor where population and occupation data were obtained on a house-to-house basis, it was found that 80% of those in wage employment were born in places outside the village and its locality, whilst those born in the locality retained their traditional occupations.

The improvement in standards of education did not have much effect on the post-school occupations of those who remained in the village. On the basis of a study of the occupations of school leavers in Battor over a period of four years, it was found that 37% of them left the village and, of the remainder, only 2% obtained regular wage employment, the majority returning to traditional occupations. Of those who left the village, half went to other rural areas where they obtained employment as apprentices, as pupil teachers, or in craft industries. The other half went to urban centres mostly for further education and training. As a general rule it appears that the creation of new employments in places of centrality does little to change the occupations of those born in the place and instead attracts people who were born elsewhere. The most important effect of new wage employments on the occupation of persons born in the place is to give them opportunities for casual, part-time work, for instance in manual labour on roads or in construction, but these are subsidiary to their traditional occupation.

The emergence of places of centrality has taken place against the general overall trend of depopulation in the area and it is likely that some 40,000 persons may have left between the two census dates, if an allowance is made for a natural population growth of about 2.6% per annum. The Censuses show a drop of population from 103,000 in 1948 to 86,000 in 1960 for the whole of the Tongu District. The cause of this loss has been mainly the migration of Tongu to new settlements upstream. The Census, undertaken by the Volta River Authority 1962—64, of those living in the area to be inundated by the Volta Lake, showed that some 20,000 Tongu were then living in the upper reaches of the Volta River (Information from Resettlement Office, Volta River Authority).

This migration of Tongu upstream for fishing has been a major feature of the riparian economy for many generations and Tongu can be found fishing in inland waters over a wide area in West Africa (Lawson, 1958, p. 21). The migration, which fishermen start as an annual occurrence, frequently leads to permanent emigration from the Lower Volta but traditional ties with the home village are maintained, though these links appear to be getting more tenuous, as evidenced by the smaller participation since 1954 of migrants in festivities, traditional ceremonies, and funerals, and in sending the dead for burial to the ancestral home village.

It seems probable however that, before 1964, the movement of fishermen upstream was declining due to new employment opportunities which were then available in the larger villages of the Lower Volta, which reduced the economic importance of annual migration for fishing, which had hitherto provided a substantial source of income. Since 1964 when the Volta Lake began to form, the prolific fisheries which developed also led to a considerable seasonal movement of fishermen from the Lower Volta to Akosombo and places on the Lake. In Battor for example, for a few months in 1966 and 1967, all the able bodied men except those in wage employment left to fish in the Lake. It seems probable that, for some, this temporary migration to the Lake will develop into more permanent settlement as the Lake fisheries stabilise.

Throughout the decade there does not appear to have been any large scale movement of people from the Tongu District to towns and cities outside and the movement from one rural environment to another has been more important than the rural-urban movement.

iii. *Occupational changes between 1948 and 1967*
Data on occupational structure are available from the 1960 but not the 1948 Census. Some indication of the changes in occupation can, however, be obtained from data for Battor and for other large villages in the district. Data for Battor are given in Table 4.
It must be noted that the 1964 occupational structure of Battor differs significantly from the structure of the Tongu District as given in the 1960 Census. The most important differences are in the smaller proportion engaged in agriculture (61% in Battor compared to 76% in Tongu District) and the higher proportion engaged in 'other services' (16%

TABLE 4

Occupational structure of Tongu District and Battor (main occupations only) as percent of total occupations

	All Tongu District 1960 Census	Battor 1954	Battor 1964 (Mid)**
All employed persons*	38,000	359	368
	% of total	% of total	
Agriculture			
Field crops	63	36	54
Cocoa	4	–	–
Livestock	2	–	–
Other	–	–	–
Fishing	7	39	7
Total for agriculture	76	75	61
Manufacturing	8	6	8
Construction	2	–	–
Commerce	10	10	15
Other services	4	9	16

* 'Employed persons' are defined as 'working persons' in the 1960 Census (See Vol. III, p. xv). The category covers those working for wages, those self employed, those undertaking seasonal work and also subsistence farmers.

** By the end of 1964 many farmers had gone to fish in the Volta Lake. Fishing then exceeded farming as the main occupation and source of income for persons in Battor.

compared with 4%). Nearly all those engaged in 'other services' are engaged in wage employment which provides a regular source of income throughout the year and it seems likely that, as will be described later, such persons have a significant role to play in the process of rural economic growth.

In 1954 most occupations were concerned with subsistence production of fish, clams and crops. In outlying hamlets probably some 70%–75% of production was for domestic consumption. In larger villages where there were some self-employed craftsmen and wage-earners, the subsistence portion of aggregate village real income was as low as 30% though for many households, i.e. excluding non-farming households, it would probably average at least 60%. Most households had more than one source of income, usually from farming and fishing, which involved two peak seasons of labour input. At least half the population of the Lower Volta considered farming and fishing to be their main occupations and most other persons considered them as secondary occupations.

Most adults in 1954 had more than one occupation. Some form of farming for subsistence was carried on throughout the year but most non-agricultural work was highly seasonal. In particular both up-river fishing and clam diving occurred between late November and early June. Certain cash crops were also highly seasonal, e.g. sweet potato, groundnut and maize which were harvested mainly in February and in August, most for immediate sale, very little being stored on the farm. The processing of cassava by drying to make *kokonte* provided a further seasonal source of income and this was exported in bulk particularly during the early floods from August onwards. In 1954, little savings were made, with one or two exceptions, and nearly all individuals struggled throughout the year to obtain a continuous supply of cash to meet day to day requirements. This involved undertaking diverse occupations at different times of the year. Thus a woman who considered clam diving to provide the largest portion of cash income might, when this season was over, turn to petty trading or to processing cassava and selling surplus farm produce or to small craft work. Other sources of small cash income were cotton spinning, native soap making, gin distilling, basket work and the manufacture of fish traps and nets. Women collected firewood and carried it up to 15 miles to the main Accra–Ada road for sale. In the Lower Volta there were and still are two highly localised and specialised industries, the pottery industry at Vume near Tefle which uses local clays and is undertaken entirely by women and the weaving industry in the hinterland of Adidome. No separate study of these industries was made since they were not typical sources of income of the riparian communities, but both increased in output over the period.

Certain occupations were studied in 1954 and 1964 including fishing in the creeks and main stream of the river, traditional agriculture, diving for clams, which was undertaken by women all along this stretch of the river. In 1954, these together probably provided some 75% of total real income of the entire riparian population and are described in more detail later.

The occupational structure of Battor differs from that of the whole Tongu District mainly in respect of the proportion engaged in services, particularly hospitals and local government and it is these which give Battor the characteristics of a 'place of centrality'. Between 1954–64 there was a slight increase in numbers employed in manufacturing as tailors and seamstresses, to supply the greater demand for clothing, especially school uniforms, and also as carpenters and masons to service the increased building activity. There was no other industry in Battor and no modern industry existed in the Tongu District in 1954.

By 1964 the occupational structure in Battor had developed certain features which could be considered characteristic of a period of rural transition, notably greater labour mobility between different occupations, increased diversity in occupations and simultaneously, the persistence of subsistence farming.

A striking change shown in Table 4 is the larger number engaged in agriculture and fewer in fishing. In 1964 however the percentages given in the table do not adequately reflect the entire situation since only main occupations are covered. Nearly all persons had at least one subsidiary occupation, the usual combination being farming and fishing, between which there was great labour mobility. By 1967 fishing was dominant over farming as a main occupation and source of income.

In 1964 there were on average 2.2 different sources of income per household compared to 1.4 in 1954. New sources of income in 1964 came partly from new wage employment associated with investment originating from outside the area, such as government spending on education and health. There were also new occupations in the traditional sector, such as collecting shells for glass making, breaking stones, collecting sand for building, and these, though providing only subsidiary sources of income, were highly sought after.

The most important source of occupational change occurring in the Lower Volta has been the amount of investment from external sources which has had certain multiplier and linkage effects in creating and expanding wage employment. The numbers employed for wages in the larger villages have increased and the proportion engaged in agriculture decreased. This has been most pronounced in Sogakope, Adidome and Tefle where the 1960 Census gave non-agricultural employments as 75% of total. In Battor, payments to wage and salary earners doubled between 1954 to 1964 and in 1964 formed 25% of aggregate village income.

The increased cash made available from wage employment has had a stimulating effect on the production of local foodstuffs for the market. This, together with investment in improving roads, has encouraged the development of local markets, notably at Aveyime, Adidome and Sogakope which serve as collecting centres for local produce. These are now regularly visited by collecting traders from Tema, Accra, Koforidua. Increases in road traffic has had a small multiplier effect in creating employment for fitters, motor mechanics, service stations and drivers. Improved social services have led to a higher level of demand for certain imported goods, such as medicines, health and hygiene requirements, baby foods, school books, uniforms, shoes, etc., and some demands have had a local multiplier effect in creating work for small craftsmen, e.g. tailors, seamstresses, carpenters.

Investment in infrastructure, social services, etc. in the Lower Volta not only created new full time wage employments but also enabled those employed in traditional occupations as farmers and fishermen to take part time and temporary employment. This has enabled individuals and households to have a greater diversity in sources of income. Such diversity in occupations has many advantages. It gives the individual a greater security of income in conditions of economic change, providing a hedge against loss of crops due to poor harvests. This is particularly desirable for persons who are engaged in primary production especially when farming is subject to unforeseen hazards such as waterlogging due to rains and floods. It also gives the individual greater personal physical mobility. He is less tied to one place, one job, one employer and is thus able to adjust his work to other demands made on his time, especially his traditional occupation.

Labour demands of the farm, especially for subsistence, take priority over all other work. Where full time wage employment was taken it was not unusual for the employee to take time off for farm work at the period of peak farm labour input, i.e. at planting time. This indicates there would be a fuller utilisation of labour resources if new wage employment were phased to alternate with the seasons of heavy farm labour input. Where casual wage employment and subsistence farming are competing and not complementary employments, farm work retains precedence. There is still a seasonal variation in employment and income but diversity in employments now available has somewhat decreased this variation. In spite of new sources of income however there are nearly as many people now engaged in farming as a subsidiary source of income, as previously. The tradition of providing the household with subsistence staples, has not diminished.

Casual wage employments pay different wages for unskilled labour at different times of the year thus demonstrating a seasonal variability in the marginal productivity of labour. The wage determinant is generally the demand for labour in agriculture though after 1964 the level was set by earnings from fisheries. For example unskilled labour employed on stone breaking and sand collecting during a period of slack farming received 3/- per day in 1964. During 1965 however, when many men were engaged in lake fishing, a privately employed labourer could receive 6/6 to 7/6 per day. An increase in diversity of employment tends to even out seasonal differences in the marginal productivity of labour, and in cash incomes.

There is, at the moment, insufficient demand to induce complete specialisation in rural employment. Thus a tailor or seamstress undertakes fishing or farming or even unskilled labouring work when not engaged on the main occupation. Teachers and clerks engaged by the local authority may have other sources of income, and, if they can get land, may undertake subsistence farming.

The riparian people of the Lower Volta must still be considered as mainly farmers and fishermen with a high degree of mobility between these two occupations. In 1964 most income was obtained from farming but in 1965—67, fishing in the Lake to which most adults migrated, formed the main source of income. Any development in agriculture in this region in the future must consider its opportunity costs to be determined by earnings from fishing. Failure to recognise this led to disappointing production results in the Asuchari area near Amedica where, it was expected, large numbers of farmers would turn to sugar cane farming to supply the nearby sugar refinery, but they have found fishing to be more recently attractive.

2   Agriculture

i.   *Agriculture in 1954*

Agriculture provided the most important source of cash income in the Lower Volta in 1954 equal to around £25 per annum per household (at current prices) or about 70% of aggregate real income. There was, of course, some variation in the size of output per household, depending mostly on the amount of labour involved. There was no shortage of land in 1954 and this did not operate as a constraint to production. There were very few wealthy land-owning and farming households. They either owned palm oil plantations or land or creeks which were subject to annual flooding and which were valuable for fishing. The main crops which continue to be grown are cassava, groundnuts, maize and sweet potato. In 1954 upstream from Aveyime, vegetables such as okro, tomato and egg plant were grown. Sugar cane was produced in the area south of Tefle which is outside the district studied here. Though, in Battor, subsistence production totalled only some 30% of aggregate food crop production, most of the riparian population produce some 60%–70% for subsistence. This may be compared with an analysis made of Ghana National Household Expenditure data which showed that in the Volta Region as a whole, of total amount of food consumed, 47% was from sources produced by the household (Golding, 1962).

The level of agricultural production per household in Battor however is not typical of that of the wider riparian area since a much smaller proportion of households undertook agriculture and there was a wider diversity of employments than in the smaller villages and hamlets. In spite of this two thirds of the adult population of Battor undertook agricultural work in 1954 and one third considered farming to be their main occupation. No farming was carried out at all by 20% of the households, who purchased food needs locally. The heads of such households were all 'strangers' (i.e. not born in the vicinity) and were engaged in wage employment. About 40% of cassava and maize cultivated by Battor farmers was used for subsistence. Groundnuts and sweet potato were grown entirely as cash crops and, together with about one third of cassava harvested, were exported from the area.

No rotation of crops is practised but there is a land rotating system of agriculture. Crops are grown on diverse small plots of land sometimes only 0.1 acre in size. In 1954 the average plot around Battor was 0.4 acre compared with 0.65 acre in 1964, each household farming an average of three to four plots.

Farming was undertaken entirely with hoe and cutlass in 1954; no modern techniques were used. However, by 1964 a few farmers operated tractors hired from the government controlled co-operative (United Ghana Farmer's Co-operative Council) at a highly subsidised rate but, with the exception of the flatter, less porous land adjacent to the Accra plains and at certain places to the east of the Volta, very little land in this area is suitable for tractor use without much more irrigation and land clearing. These would involve considerable cost. A scheme of irrigation for the production of rice and sugar cane which was partially implemented in the area between Amedica and Aveyime by the government was estimated to involve clearing and irrigation costs of some £120 per acre (Lawson, 1963, p. 89), but this cost was eventually exceeded. After the 1966 coup the co-operative movement in Ghana was somewhat discredited owing to its political activities and, in those places where tractors continued to be offered for hire, hire charges increased to more realistic levels. At higher hiring costs their use was no longer profitable in this area. By 1967 all farmers were again entirely dependent on hoe and cutlass.

Both men and women engage in farm work and there is some traditional division of labour between them, men doing most of the heavy clearing and women the weeding. Men may help in harvesting but this is mostly done by women. Prior to the construction of the dam, there was a preference to cultivate land irrigated by floods which was quickly planted as the water retreated. Such land will be referred to here as creek land. Other land will be described as upland.

In 1954 it was commonly asserted that creek land was more fertile than upland because of silting brought by the flood. Soil tests taken from a large number of samples of each type of soil in 1954 however failed to reveal any difference in chemical composition and the difference in yields was mainly attributed to moisture content. Yields from 36 sample plots showed quite clearly that, for both groundnuts and cassava, creek land was much more productive than upland. Groundnut yields more than doubled when grown on creek land and after six months growth in creek soil cassava had a higher yield than cassava grown for 14 months on upland soil. In 1954 Battor farmers grew 65% of their crops on creek land and this proportion was typical for the whole of the riparian area. The annually flooding of the land was thus of great economic importance to agriculture.

In 1954 most households farmed a mixture of crops, some interplanted, with cassava forming the basic staple. Cassava, using 57% of land was the main crop and, as it could be stored in the ground for two to three years, it provided a food reserve. Some was processed for sale by drying to give *kokonte*. Maize and groundnuts each occupied 18% of the land under cultivation and sweet potatoes the remainder. About one tenth of all land around Battor was under cultivation at the time of the 1954 survey; this was typical of all riparian lands in the Lower Volta. Upland areas were farmed under continuous cultivation for some 3—5 years and then rested for 10 to 15 years. Creek land however was in constant use from year to year especially for groundnut cultivation. No land use study was made of lands lying beyond the riparian fringe but a very great proportion of the Accra Plains to the south and land lying to the east of the river was used for cattle ranging.

The total value of crops harvested by Battor farmers in 1954 was £3357, equal to £25 per farming household with a modal value of less than £10 and a median of £23. The mean was biased by six households which obtained a total of £621 additional income from oil palm plantations. Nearly all farm labour was from household sources. Some migrant labourers who came annually from Togoland, were employed in planting and harvesting and a total of 5% of the value of all crops harvested was used for wages in kind and cash.

Cassava was grown in creeks since it matured much more quickly and could be harvested after six to eight months. It was usual to leave it in the soil until required. When the floods rose there was often a last minute rush to retrieve cassava before the river submerged the crop. Sometimes the land flooded suddenly and it was not unusual to see farmers diving under four or five feet of water to retrieve cassava. This reluctance to harvest until actual flooding occurred caused losses every year. Even in 1954 when the flood was small, 18 farmers lost between them eight acres of cassava which would have yielded £200.

Observations made by the VRPPC indicated that farming conditions in Battor including real earnings from farming, methods and costs of production, and crop yields were typical of the whole riparian area in which at least half total agricultural earnings were obtained from crops grown on land subject to flooding annually. Oil palm plantations existed at Sikor, at the Apediwoe Islands and at Vome, yielding a total income of some £4,700 per annum.

In Battor the most important crop was cassava valued at nearly 60% of total agricultural production. It was the source of about half total cash income. In the wider riparian area however, especially near creeks, there was some specialisation in groundnuts, and some villages which lay between Aveyime and Tefle received from one-third to two-thirds of the total cash income from this source. It was obvious, in 1954, that any change in the flow of the river Volta which would reduce or prevent annual flooding would undoubtedly affect the agriculture of the Lower Volta by reducing yields from the irrigated creek land.

ii. *Agriculture changes, 1954–64*
Over the decade there was a doubling of acreage under culti-

vation in the lands owned and farmed by Battor people. Labour input appeared to have increased, mainly as a result of larger numbers employed but only slightly as a result of greater labour time per capita spent on the farm. No structural changes occurred, methods of cultivation were exactly the same as in 1954.

The changes which took place in employment in agriculture over 1954–64 are given in Table 5.

Households in which farming was carried on as a main occupation decreased from 93 in 1954 to 78 in 1964, but there was rise in the number of adults engaged mainly in agriculture, from 129 to 199. The numbers of people engaged in farming as a main and subsidiary occupation increased from 210 to 273. Between 1954–63 there was a switch from fishing to farming due to a change in comparative returns. By 1964 there were more adults per household participating in farming than previously and more specialisation in agricultural work appeared to have taken place. However the trend towards an increase in employment in agriculture which was in evidence between 1954–63 was reversed after 1964 when fisheries in the newly formed Volta Lake offered very lucrative employment. Between 1965–67 nearly all able bodied adult males, except those in regular wage employment, left Battor at some period to fish in the Lake.

The number of persons engaged in farming as a subsidiary occupation in 1964 was less than in 1954. The main reason for this was that a wider choice of employment led, by 1964, to a greater diversity in subsidiary sources of income. In 1954 each household had an average of 1.4 different sources of income compared with 2.2 in 1964.

Comparative data on agriculture for 1954 and 1964 is given in Tables 5, 6 and 7.

These tables use a new concept, that of man equivalents. It has already been stated that many people in this area have more than one source of real income, the usual combination being farming and fishing or farming and diving for clams. However, in most cases the subsidiary occupation is carried out for subsistence and not for cash income, and has a labour input which is less than that used in main occupations. It would be improper to consider all those employed in agriculture, whether as a main occupation or as a subsidiary occupation, as being equal units of man-power. The study of labour inputs showed that the average input of labour per farmer who claimed agriculture as his main employment totalled 696 hours per annum compared to 326 hours input per farmer who considered agriculture as a subsidiary employment (Lawson, 1968a, p. 57). On this basis it was estimated that on average, the labour input of the former was equal to twice that of the latter. The use of child labour has been left out of these calculations as it was found to be impossible to keep records of the activities of children. Their farming activities were most important in weeding and harvest.

Over the ten years 1954—64 land under cultivation and average size of holding per household approximately doubled in size. Each holding consisted of a number of separated plots. In 1954 though one household had thirteen separate plots, the average was three with an average plot size of 0.4 acres. In 1964 when more careful observations were taken of the changes in acreages under cultivation over the period of a year it was found that the average number of holdings varied from two to five per household during the year with an average plot size of 0.65 acres and a total holding of 2.4 acres. This may be compared to the average size of holding in the Volta Region which the Agricultural Census recorded as 3.1 acres (Agricultural Census of Ghana, 1964). It is not known however at what period of the year the Agricultural Census was taken and as there is a great seasonal variation in cultivation throughout the year, its results must be interpreted cautiously.

Total acreage under cultivation by Battor farmers rose from 116.7 acres in 1954 to 214.23 acres in 1964 i.e. by 185%. Not all this was in the immediate vicinity of Battor, one-tenth of it was across the river. The increase in demand for agricultural produce which occurred between 1954—64 induced the cultivation of what previously had been marginal land. Such land had not been sub-marginal because of fertility but because of its distance from both the farmers residence and markets and such lands were brought within the margin of cultivation by the improvements in roads and markets after 1954.

TABLE 5

Employment in agriculture 1954 and 1964

	1954	1964
Total adult population	359	368
Numbers engaged in farming as main and subsidiary occupation	210	273
Numbers engaged in farming as main occupation	129	199
Numbers engaged in farming as a subsidiary occupation	81	74
Total man-equivalents engaged in agriculture	169	236
Numbers of households with at least one adult engaged in farming as a main occupation	93	78
The above expressed as a % of total number of households in village.*	81%	62%

* One person undertaking farming as a subsidiary occupation is taken to equal one half a man-equivalent.

TABLE 6

End use of agricultural output in 1954 and 1964
(£ are Ghana £)

	1954	1964
1. Total value of output including home consumption.	£3,978	£10,700
2. Of which (a) Consumed by household (subsistence)	£1,300	£ 4,565
(b) Paid for labour in kind	—	£ 1,135
(c) Paid for labour in cash	£ 117	£ 20
3. Value of cash sales proceeds (1−2(a) and 2(b)).	£2,678	£ 5,000
4. Aggregate net cash earnings (3−2(c))	£2,561	£ 4,990
5. Subsistence as % of total value off output.	33%	44%
6. Subsistence per man equivalent (allowing for price rise, see 9. below)	£8	£17
7. Labour costs as % of total value of output	2%	10%
8. Net cash earnings as % of total value of output	60%	47%
9. Index of prices of local foodstuffs*	100	185

* Based on Index of Prices of Local Foodstuffs at Ho, Volta Region, collected by Central Bureau of Statistics.

TABLE 7

Comparative data on agriculture over 1310 acres in the vicinity of Battor* 1954 and 1964

		1954	1964
1.	Aggregate village income from agriculture	£3,978	£10,700
2.	Total acreage of land under crops	116.7 acres	214.23 acres
3.	Percentage use of land under crops (c.f. total acreage of 1310 acres)	9%	16.3%
4.	Index of land under crops, 1954=100	100	185
5.	Man equivalents involved in farming	169	236
6.	Average size of holdings per household	1.2 acres	2.4 acres
7.	Average acreage per man equivalent	.75 acres	.9 acres
8.	Average value of off-take per acre	£34	£50
9.	Income per household from crops	£30	£139
10.	Income per man-equivalent from crops	£23.5	£46
11.	Index of prices for local foodstuffs (prices taken as at Ho, 1954=100)	100	185
12.	Index of value of off-take per acre allowing for price increases as above.**	100	80
13.	Index of incomes per man-equivalent employed allowing for prices increases as above.***	100	106

* Area covered is mapped in the F.A.O. Lower Flood Plain Survey, 1962, as areas 13 and 19, with a total average of 1310 acres).

** Indicates a diminishing return to land.

*** Indicates a slight increase in productivity per man-equivalent but this has not been due to any improvements in technique but to slightly longer hours worked.

38 THE CHANGING ECONOMY OF THE LOWER VOLTA

The intensity of riparian land under cultivation, recorded over the whole stretch of the river between Tefle and Senchi in 1954 was 10%. By 1964 this intensity of cultivation had increased and around Battor had reached about 20% which, on the evidence given here is probably above optimum and may be compared with the national average of 10% (Agricultural Census of Ghana, 1964).

A study was made in 1964 of the use of labour of members of farming households. The study covered a representative sample of 28% of the total number of farming households in Battor and records were taken daily over 16 months, though only 12 months were used for analysis. More detailed results of this study have been published elsewhere (Lawson, 1968a, p. 58). Farmers in the sample worked an average of 174 days on the farm over the year. There was, however, a certain amount of variation in labour input with a range, in days worked per year, of 136–245 days and a mean deviation from the mean of 28. Taking the samples as a whole the average time spent over the year on different activities by those who recorded their main source of income as arising from farming were computed and are recorded below:

Use of Time		Days spent
Work on farm		174 days
Resting	53½	
Sundays	25	84
Stayed at home because of rain	5½	
Attended funerals		28
Travelling and visiting the market *		28
Fishing		13½
Communal labour		12½
Farmer sick	9½	10½
Family sick	1	
Work on house construction		6½
Visited market		3
Attended courts		2
Attended celebrations		2
Others		1
Total		365 days

* These two were not always differentiated since sometimes the market would be visited at Aveyime en route for distant destinations, and sometimes distant markets would be visited whilst 'travelling'.

Some of the activities listed above can be considered of economic value and productive of 'Z' goods, i.e. non-farm goods such as communal labour, house building, fishing and marketing and, adding these to the time spent on agriculture, farmers were engaged on economic activities on some 205 days per year.

Apart from the farmer, however, relatives and some paid labourers, who considered farming as a subsidiary occupation, also did farm work, contributing an average labour input of 426 hours to the household farming unit. Thus the main farmer's input provided about 60% of total, 40% of labour input being provided by other persons, mostly adult female relatives and wives. A small amount of child labour was used but only at week-ends and during holidays from school and no children in the village were deliberately kept away from school to help in farm work or in any other economic activity though there were reports of this happening in the outlying hamlets. Though in 1954 no detailed records were taken of labour input into farming, it was obvious that children then played a significant role. Few children attended school and the older ones usually accompanied their parents on their daily tasks.

The low daily average level of labour input into farming is largely a function of high seasonal variation in the labour requirements of traditional farming. Here the main labour requirement is at planting season, lasting for some four to six weeks in April and May. Labour requirements fall off after that since less labour is required for weeding though there is a lower peak demand for labour at harvest time, especially for groundnuts and maize. Failure to plant at the right time cannot be made up by additional labour input later on since planting time is determined by seasonal weather conditions. Thus the amount of labour which can be commanded at the peak planting season determines the amount of labour required at other times, i.e. for weeding and harvesting. Households consider it of prime importance to plant the staple food crop in at least sufficient quantities to meet subsistence requirements and only after then are cash crops planted.

Over the year the number of days per month on which

farm work was undertaken by those considering farming as their main source of income varied from 10 to 22 with an average of 14 days per month. An average of 3.1 hours per day were worked. Spreading this over a normal working month of, say, 24 days per month, the average daily input by such a farmer into agriculture is only 2.4 hours. Other farming assistants, mainly family labour, put in an average of 35 hours per month, compared to the farmer's 58 hours. This is probably a higher level of total family labour input than in 1954. Comparisons of labour input into traditional agriculture made with other tropical countries show that the findings here are not very different from those found in other similar studies elsewhere in Africa where there is a high seasonal input and labour input averages around 700–800 hours per year in food farming (Lawson, 1968a, p. 58, Haswell, 1963; Beckett, 1947; Baldwin, 1957; Galletti, Baldwin and Dina, 1956).

Records were kept of all other inputs which mostly included the cost of implements, seeds, and 'plantings' i.e. cassava sticks and sweet potato shoots. These inputs averaged £5 per household, equivalent to 3.6% of the value of output. Comparisons with other West African countries are given in Table 8. The figure for Battor is below the average for Ghana computed for 1960 at 4.6% but is considerably higher than that of most other West African countries.

Some significant conclusions were drawn from this comparative study of agriculture in 1954–64. There was probably very little increase in labour productivity and this barely compensated for the loss of child labour. There was a diminishing return to land by 1964 especially on land adjacent to villages. There was a wider range of earnings from agriculture. The level of subsistence appeared to have increased slightly over 1954, and this was reflected in a better level of nutrition. These four conclusions are discussed in greater detail below.

iii. *Labour productivity*
The productivity of labour appears from the tables to have increased slightly by some 6% between 1954 and 1964. This however was not due to any improvement in techniques but

TABLE 8

Non-labour inputs into agriculture as a percent of total output

Country	Date of Records	Non-labour input as % of output
Ivory Coast	1964	8.5
Niger	1956	.9
Chad	1956	1.5
Central African Republic	1961	3.7
Upper Volta	1956	1.2
Ghana (Battor)	1964–5	3.6
Ghana*	1960	4.6

Source: E.C.A. Statistical Bulletin for Africa, 1965 Part 2 (except Ghana data).

* The ratio of non-labour input to output can be compared with figures for agriculture for all Ghana which may be computed from estimates of capital stock at mid 1960 and the value of agricultural output for 1960. The estimate of rural capital stock other than investment in cocoa, livestock and canoes was £2.6 million with an addition of £1.4 million in agricultural machinery. The total of £4 million may be compared with total output from the agricultural sector in 1960 of £87.9 and from this can be computed the ratio of non-labour input to output of 4.6%. This ratio may have increased somewhat since then as there has been a certain amount of input of agricultural machinery into State and Workers Brigade Farms since 1960, though it is unlikely that this has had much effect on increasing agricultural production. (Figures estimated from National Accounts and Economic Survey, 1960. Central Bureau of Statistics, Accra).

to a slightly higher labour input. It must be noted however that the increase in labour productivity of 6% probably does not compensate for the loss of child labour which, since 1960 has been conpulsorily diverted into education. School children can no longer spend much time on farm work. Previously a child of 10 to 14 years could probably equal half an adult in terms of labour input into agriculture. Estimates of child labour force in Battor in 1954 indicated that they could have been responsible for some 5%–7% of aggregate agricultural production. As child labour has been almost eliminated from farm work an increase of at least 7% in the labour productivity of adult farmers would be needed to compensate for this loss.

iv. Diminishing return to land

By 1964 the return to land had diminished by at least 20%, particularly on land around Battor, due to the over intensive use of the land which had increased from 10% in 1954 to 20% in 1964. An aerial photograph taken in 1959 showed the area round Battor to be a solid mosaic of farm plots with mainly only creeks and water logged areas not under farm use. To the south of Battor the use of land for crop farming was limited by the poor soils of the Accra Plains. Diminishing returns to land could not be shown on lands lying across the river since most of these had not been in production for very long and there was no shortage of available land. In the Battor area however the level of land utilisation is probably greatly above optimum since it does not allow adequate time for resting to restore fertility. An adequate period is professionally considered to be between four and five times the length of time land has been under cultivation.

v. Earnings

A wider range in household earnings from agriculture in 1964 was evident as the following distribution illustrates.

TABLE 9

Comparisons of real earnings from agriculture 1954 and 1964, in Battor *

Gross annual value of real earnings in £'s	1954 % of households	1964 % of household
£300–350	6	10
250–299	3	
200–249	3 } 22	
150–199	–	
100–149	10	
50–99	47	40
20–49	28	50
Less than 20	3 } 31	
	100	100

* Includes value of own produce consumed plus cash earnings.

Higher earnings were a function of higher household labour input, from wives and other members of the extended family. The household with the largest production included four wives. Reliance on family labour is increasing. There was no evidence of diminishing returns to labour but this would be difficult to measure without more accurate records of the quality of work performed by each member of the household and this is particularly variable between wives, depending on their physical health and whether they are lactating or pregnant.

vi. *The level of subsistence*
Table 6 indicates a change in proportion of subsistence production to total value of off-take from 33% to 44% between 1954 and 1964. However, considering this in real terms, due allowance must be made for the 185% price increase in foodstuffs between these dates and the increased number of man-equivalents involved in farming. Allowing for these there was in fact a 15% increase in the value of crops taken off for subsistence and this was reflected in a higher consumption of food. Dietary studies undertaken in 1954 and 1965 showed an average increase in daily consumption of calories from 2615 to 2932 per man equivalent per day (Lawson, 1967b).

Over the riparian lands of the Lower Volta in 1964 similar changes to those listed above were found. Aerial photographs* taken in 1959 showed a more intensive use of land in the immediate proximity of villages and indicated a diminishing return to land, as at Battor. In 1964, field studies showed a wider use of land in areas more distant from villages which had, because of location, been previously sub-marginal. This was particularly obvious in lands on the east bank of the river. A much higher level of production of all foodstuffs had developed, particularly in cash crops. This was accompanied by a great expansion of local foodstuffs passing through markets on the way to cities. In Aveyime market a four-fold increase in the amount of local food crops appearing for sale

---
* Aerial photograph: Lower Volta Flood Plain No. 9344. December 1959. Government Survey Department.

was noted over this period. Other new markets had developed since 1954, e.g. at Sogakope and Tefle. Throughout the riparian region there had been an increase in aggregate labour input into agriculture during 1954–64, partly due to a decline in fishing.

3 Volta Fisheries

Before the Volta Lake formed the river's fisheries fell into four groups, estuarine grounds, tidal, upper, and creek fisheries. The three latter were almost entirely undertaken by Tongu who can be found fishing in inland waterways throughout West Africa. The Volta River Authority located 20,000 Tongu fishermen in 1962–3, during its census of the population of those who would be affected by the rising of the Volta Lake.

i. *The Upper Fresh Water Fisheries*
Before incorporation into the Lake these fisheries existed on stretches north of Amedica and included Volta tributaries such as the Oti, Afram and Black Volta Rivers. These were of great economic significance to people of the Lower Volta especially those from Mafe, Mepe, Bakpa, Tefle and Battor, from which probably some 1000 to 1500 fishermen and their families migrated each year between November and July or August, returning downstream to undertake seasonal farming. This annual migration had, in many cases, led to a permanent resettlement of Tongu in the upper reaches where they lived in widely scattered villages and practised subsistence agriculture (Lawson, 1958, p. 25).

In Battor for example in 1954, 81 men (out of 353 total adult males) and 21 women were fishing upstream and all were expected to return before September. In fact less than half returned and though various explanations for this were given by their relatives it was obvious that ties with Battor were becoming increasingly tenuous. In hamlets surrounding Battor some 157 men and 127 women returned out of a likely annual migration from the Battor area of some 400 to 500 adults.

Incomes earned from fishing were generally low, except for about 15 men who owned seine nets. Statistics of catches taken by the Fisheries Department for the years 1948–51 gave an average annual landing of 6 tons per seine with a high variation from year to year (Reports of Government Fisheries Department, Accra, 1948–52). In an average year seine nets may have landed catches worth some £8000 in total. Four seine net owners living in Battor in 1954 gave the average value of fish caught in their nets as £400, £150, £600 and £650 respectively.

Thirty six fishermen returned to Battor from fishing upstream in 1954 having earned a total of £1846 equal to about £50 per head. The main capital costs of fishing in 1954 were in seine nets, valued at £800 for four; other equipment consisted of 24 canoes, 133 set nets, 152 lines, over a thousand basket traps and many cast nets. The distribution of ownership of fisheries capital is given in Table 10. No data on fisheries capital are available for 1964.

TABLE 10

The distribution of capital and earnings (from sales) between 36 fishermen in 1954 and 50 fishermen in 1964

Value of fisheries capital, and earnings from fishing	No. of fishermen owning this value of gear	No. of fishermen having this level of gross earnings	
£'s	1954	1954	1964
0–49	23	22	17
50–99	8	3	25
100–149	1	21	2
150–199	–	6	2
200–299	2	4	–
300–399	–	–	4
400–499	1	–	–
500–599	1	–	–

Only ten men owned fishing capital worth over £150. There was a high correlation between capital owned and income received by fishermen. Only seine net owners earned a reasonable income from fishing, most earning less than £50.

Ten earned less than £10. It must be noted that earnings quoted above represent net surplus remaining after living expenses had been provided for upstream. Earnings of seine nets are traditionally divided between net owners and all those who comprised the 'company', usually some 8 fishermen. Net owners take two-thirds of net earnings. This has to cover repairs and costs of providing subsistence for the company. The remaining one-third is shared equally between all fishermen.

Most fishermen incur debts before going up river in November, repaying on their return the following July or August. If however fishermen do not earn enough to repay debts they usually stay up river. In Battor, out of a total of 36 fishers, 27 were in debt at the commencement of the 1953–54 season and all except eight were able to repay in full on their return downstream. Average debts at commencement of the 1953–4 season were £40 but there were six very large debts of between £50 and £150. Most debts were small, (17 men had borrowed £10 or less) usually being incurred to cover travelling and living expenses until they started receiving cash from fish sales. It was commonly stated that interest charged on loans in the region was at the rate of 50 per cent, but this did not occur amongst fishermen. Out of 27 fishermen only nine paid any interest at all at rates varying from 3% to 25% per annum. Often the amount to be repaid was calculated at 50% higher than principal but borrowers were given periods of up to six years in which to repay which would be equal to a compound rate of interest of 7% per annum. Others borrowed mostly from relatives when small amounts up to £10 were involved and no interest was charged. After deducting repayments of loans from average earnings of £50 in 1954 the net sum remaining averaged £34 per fisherman.

Fishermen lived an almost hand-to-mouth existence, borrowing money at commencement of season and repaying at the end if they were able. Most fishermen brought little money downstream and most of this was spent on drinks to celebrate their home-coming, though a smaller amount was also used in farming and house construction.

The value of upstream fisheries to most seasonally

migrating Tongu appeared to be largely in providing them with subsistence during a period when they would be otherwise unoccupied and with the chance of earning a windfall in an exceptional season. Net earnings with which they returned were soon used in subsistence downstream and in the customary festivities accompanying their return. Only seine net owners obtained a surplus sufficient to allow for savings, and though part of this was dissipated by various family demands, some savings did accumulate from this source between 1954–64.

ii. *The Tidal Fresh-Water Fisheries and Creek Fisheries*
These fisheries lie mainly between Amedica and Tefle. South of Tefle to the coast there is little fishing due to brackishness. Before the Lake filled the 32 mile stretch from Tefle to Amedica had a clear sandy bed with only a few rocky outcrops. The most important fishing on this stretch was by seine, varying from 11–17 nets per year. Set nets were not much used.

Between 1945 and 1952 the Fisheries Department kept records of hauls and catches of two seine nets which were operated at Adidome and Volo, both within five miles of Battor. Great variation in annual catches from 5 to 50 tons occurred, mainly due to the unexplained variation in populations of *Chrysichthys sp.*, which contributed more than 80 per cent to total seine landings (Report of Government Fisheries Department, 1951–2). During good years, large quantities of fish were probably exported from the area, but in 1954, an average year, fish caught in this stretch of the river was entirely consumed locally and much was used for subsistence. In 1954, fishing in the tidal fresh water stretch yielded an income of £161 to Battor, and creeks which had been flooded to an average level that year yielded a further £300. Fishing in both these locations was undertaken for subsistence also.

Total net earnings from fishing in the Battor area in 1954 was £2350. In 1964 fishing earnings increased considerably to £8314 though only 24 out of the 50 men recorded actually lived in Battor village. The high 1964 earnings were due to the exceptional floods of 1963 and the resulting prolific creek fishery. River fishing was however insignificant. Forty-one men fished almost continuously in creeks near to Battor during the months January-November 1964, and nine less regularly in river and creeks. Average labour input per man into fishing was 839 hours over the 11 months, though this did not include time spent mending nets which could have added a further 300 hours. This is higher than labour input into farming which, as already noted, is highly seasonal. A considerable amount of fish was exported from the area during 1964 and average per capita real earnings were £166 of which fish worth £74 were used for subsistence, fish sales amounting to £92. Exceptional income due to the abnormal conditions of 1964 was estimated to be £3000, based on the value of fish taken from creeks not normally flooded.

The distribution of income between the 50 fishermen in 1964 is compared with the 36 fishermen of 1954 in Table 11 below. Table 12 gives the labour input of fishermen in the 1964 season.

Only four seine net owners earned high incomes from fishing. Most men received net cash incomes of less than £100. Earnings from fishing are much more varied from year to year than agriculture and it would be difficult to generalise

TABLE 11

Distribution of earnings from fishing in 1954 (between 36 men) and 1964 (between 50 men)*

	1954	1964	
Income level	Distribution of net cash income (no subsistence data)	Distribution of earnings (sub- sistence + sales)	Distribution of net cash income
£0–£49	22	9	17
£50–£99	3	6	25
£100–149	1	10	2
£150–£199	6	18	2
£200–£249	4	2	–
£250–£299	–	–	–
£300–£349	–	1	–
£300–£399	–	–	4
Over 400	–	4	–

* Not all these men lived in Battor.

TABLE 12

Distribution of labour input into fishing in 1964

Hours input over 11 months	No. of men
0– 200 hours	6
200– 400	3
400– 600	7
600– 800	6
800–1000	13
1000–1200	8
1200–1400	2
1400–1600	–
1600–1800	3
1800–2000	–
2000–2200	2
Total no. of fishermen	50

on any increase in labour productivity since labour input depends on the fish population and no explanation for the variability of the dominant fish species has yet been found. Years of favourable river conditions induce a high labour input. Creeks are normally fished until they have dried out and stocks removed. The development of a more efficient fishery in the few creeks remaining in this area now the river no longer floods will depend on the development of fish-pond techniques. Until then the Lake fishery will continue to attract large numbers of migrant fishermen from the Lower Volta.

The growth pattern of new lake fisheries in Africa has however shown some fall off after an initial period of three to five years and there is already some evidence that this is happening in the Volta Lake (Petr, 1967). How this will affect the recently settled migrants from the Lower Volta is not certain.

4 The Clam Industry

This is the third most important industry on this stretch of the Lower Volta and is located between Torgome and Tefle. In 1954 it provided an aggregate yield worth over £100,000, but yields were dependent on floods and flow of the river (Purchon, 1963, p. 253). Between 1954 and 1963 some decline in the industry had taken place in preference to farming and casual wage employment, though it continued to be important to supply household subsistence needs. In 1964–65 the industry was temporarily revitalised by the change in the flow of the river and an exceptional yield was obtained. By the end of 1965, when the completion of the dam seriously affected the flow of the river downstream, it declined considerably and by 1967 had almost disappeared from this stretch of the river.

In 1964 the industry provided the main occupation for 1000 to 2000 women and a subsidiary occupation for a further 100 women who fish for subsistence. The principal beds lay in shallow water close to the river's banks. A few sand banks and shallow stretches mid-stream also provided further beds, though these shifted slightly from year to year. The most important beds were those upstream near Akuse at Torgome, Asuchari, Alaboke, Volivoe and Duffor where clams were transplanted in 'farms'. Research by the Fisheries Department reported a more rapid growth rate of clams kept in this condition which yielded a growth in overall weight of 60% in four months.

The clams (*Egeria radiata*) are gathered at an average depth of about 2 metres. Before the dam was constructed the gathering of clams commenced usually from December, as soon as the flood flow had subsided and the water became clear, and continued until the river rose again in July. Clams are collected by hand from the bed of the river by women who dive from narrow dugout canoes, working continuously for three to four hours a day at low tide. Part of the catch is then transplanted in shallower areas near the banks of the river in 'farms' marked out on the river by sticks where clams grow rapidly. Like the harvesting of cassava mentioned earlier, clams are finally collected from 'farms' in a general panic just as the flood rises in June and July.

Over half the women engaged in clam fishing in 1954 owned canoes, which were traditional marriage gifts from husband to wife, costing from £G2 to £G12 depending on size, and representing the main capital input in the industry. Other items were pans, baskets and paddles, which together amounted to no more than £G1. The total capital input into the industry in 1954 was estimated at £10,000 with a depreciation rate of 10% per annum (Lawson, 1963, p. 285).

At Battor, in 1954, about half the adult females dived for clams and two thirds considered it as their main source of income. Subsistence production was more common in the lower section of this stretch of the river, but upstream near the main market at Akuse, it was largely undertaken as a full-time occupation during the season. The greater growth rate of clams in the upper section of this stretch of the river induced a seasonal migration of women from downstream. Upstream, women settled in temporary camps, living in palm-frond huts with others from the same villages, returning to the same place each year.

Seasonal differences from year to year occurred, depending on the timing and height of the previous year's flood. Differences in income between clam divers depended on whether they transplanted in farms, engaged in clam trade, and on time spent in the river. In 1954, Battor women working locally earned an average of £20 per head over the season but those who, in addition, collected and traded clams in Aveyime market earned a further £3. 10s. A sample of 93 women who cultivated clam 'farms' upstream earned an average of £27 over the 1954 season and, in addition, used clams worth £6 for home consumption, thus giving a real income of £33.

The industry upstream was sufficiently prolific to support a large number of traders, most of whom were also clam divers. These women were able to add a further £11 to their income by their wholesaling function. In the 1956 season the Fisheries Department recorded that women landed 4.4 tons of clams per head including weight of shell, yielding each an income of £61 (Data from Fisheries Department, Accra). These women were however described as 'experienced and skilful and gave their full time to the work; their results were probably well above average.' A similar study undertaken by the Fisheries Department in 1956–57 season showed an average income of £70 per head.

In calculating earnings however it is important to note that there were seasonal differences in prices and that prices varied along the river. For example, prices varied from 1½d per two pound pan of fresh clams at the river side to 6d per pan later on when alternative sources of protein, especially freshwater fish, were scarce. It should be noted that clams greatly improved in quality as the season progressed, being tough and stringy at the beginning, and tender and succulent later on. To some extent the higher price towards the end of the season reflected an improved product. Large baskets of smoked clams which cost £2. 12. 6d downstream, sold at prices up to £G6 at the riverside markets of Akuse and also at Accra. There was quick variation in price in response to demand and supply conditions. Buying was undertaken by collecting traders from Accra, Somanya and Koforidua, who could make from 40% to 60% profit on cost price. Though trading was highly competitive in 1954, by 1964 there was some indication of price fixing between clam sellers.

The number of women diving for clams per day throughout the season averaged 1515 in 1954, 1400 in 1956, and 1181 in 1957, a year of little industry. In addition to these numbers there would be many others who worked only occasionally for subsistence. The 1960 Census records 2360 female fisherwomen in the Volta and Eastern Region; most of these women would be involved in clam fishing since other types of fishing are traditionally male occupations. In 1964–65 many more women were involved and bi-monthly counts averaged 1702, with a peak of 1976 women. 1964 and early 1965 were exceptionally good periods for clams and, since the river had ceased to flood, diving continued throughout the year. Yields in 1964 were exceptionally high, but by the end of 1965 fell off very rapidly. However, prices doubled and incomes from clam fishing remained high. By the end of 1965 only 18 women were diving for clams at Battor compared to 76 earlier.

Differences in clam production between 1954 and 1964 are recorded below:

TABLE 13

Differences in clam production, 1954—1964

	1954	1964
Average number of women diving for clams per day March—July; all Lower Volta.	1515*	1702
Data for Battor		
Numbers engaged as main occupation	39	61
Numbers engaged as subsidiary occupation	72	15
Numbers transplanting clams in farms upstream	15	24
Numbers engaged in wholesale trade in addition to clam diving	12	16 of which 6 trading on large scale
Average number of women in river per day	41	56
Total capital input	£ 98	£ 158
Aggregate annual cash income from clams	£500	£1790
Value of clams used for subsistence	£500	£ 814
Average income of those diving for clams as a main occupation	£ 14*	£ 48
Index of quantities produced, 1954=100	100	170
Estimated income due to exceptional conditions of the river in 1964—5 **	—	£1050

* Fishing for clams took place during 7 months only in 1954 owing to annual floods.
** Fishing took place over 12 months.

The noticeable changes in 1964 were the following:

1. Trade had increased in scale. A small number of dominant traders had emerged, all of whom were also clam fishers though they spent most time on trade. This division of labour had been emerging for some years. The tendency was noted in 1954 but the larger quantities handled in 1964 hastened this trend.

2. Cash income obtained from clams in 1964 had increased over three times from 1954. This was largely due to the extended season but also because more women had become clam 'farmers', reaping benefits of higher seasonal prices by postponing sales until clams became scarce. Greater short term capital was thus involved in the industry. Owing to increasing scarcity, clam prices, which had been only slightly greater than 1954 levels, rose steeply towards the end of 1964 and by the end of 1965 were twice the early 1964 price. The expansion of the industry in 1964 demonstrated a high labour mobility from a subsidiary to a main occupation.

3. Increased earnings obtained in 1964 had some interesting repercussions on the economic organisation of the family. Clam diving is traditionally a woman's occupation with which she is expected to provide subsistence needs of the household, using any surplus to meet her domestic obligations. Clam fishers are however also expected to assist in farm work to support the household in staples and also to help the husband on other farms when required. However in 1964 increased earnings from clam diving induced women to exploit this windfall by spending more time on clam diving and much less on farm work, whilst at the same time retaining the windfall surplus earnings for themselves. The loss of labour on household farms had, in some cases, to be made up by members of the extended family who were paid in kind and given subsistence, thus in effect, reducing the surplus available to the husband. This thus posed another threat to the stability of the traditional household and the culturally determined roles of various members.

Since the completion of the dam the river flow has stabilised and former seasonal variations have averaged out to an even annual flow. This has had the effect of moving the critical salinity boundary, on which the clam depends, downstream to 16 miles below Tefle, to within six miles of the sea (Pople and Rogoyska, 1969). If the industry is to survive it must be relocated in this area. Given the extremely mobile labour resources, there seems no reason why this should not replace the fishery which had hitherto existed further upstream.

5   Cattle

Cattle belonging to the riparian people of the Lower Volta are mostly kept in herds which graze on the east bank of the river. Very few riparian people apart from the Ada and others living south of Tefle own cattle which graze on the Accra Plains. According to records kept by the Animal Health section of the Ministry of Agriculture there were 22,397 head of cattle in 1953 in the area lying between Volo and Sogakope. By 1963 this had increased by 50% to 33,845. The annual take off in 1954 was estimated to be about 10%. Even allowing for this, plus the high mortality rate, the increase indicated above is well within the natural rate of increase.

Cattle are kept in herds varying in size from 30 to 300 and are managed in kraals kept by herdsmen, usually Fulani or Hausa. Herds contain cattle owned by a number of people, sometimes up to 20 or 30 individuals, some of whom are not known by correct name to the herdsman. The herdsman is not paid in cash for his services but takes one calf in every three born to the heifer and all the milk which is then processed into cheese. The level of husbandry is very low. Blair reporting in 1963 (FAO Report No. 1627, 1963) stated that 'most of the herds are confined to the kraal for long periods each day. Many do not leave the kraal until 9.30 or 10 a.m. and return at 4.30 to 5 p.m. Grazing time is thus limited to about 8 hours per day'. In addition, cattle may lose up to 10% in weight during the dry season. A large number of cattle are lost through careless husbandry. Some kraals are veritable seas of mud in the rainy season and common explanations givens for the death of cattle are, 'It got stuck in the mud', or 'It got drowned', 'It died of snake bite'. Other causes of fatality were mainly dysentry and castration. Cattle owners visit cattle very infrequently, sometimes only once a year, and some owners suspect that herdsmen dispose of their cattle in other ways for their own ends. No proof of this was found.

In an attempt to investigate the pattern and motivation of cattle ownership a random sample of 5% of cattle population was studied, comprising eleven herds on the east bank. All the herdsmen and 26 cattle owners were interviewed. All owners lived some distance from the kraal, some up to 40 miles away and, as kraals were generally inaccessible by road, they rarely visited them. Owners had very little practical knowledge of their cattle and received a low price for them when sold. Sales are made to itinerant dealers who ply the area from Akuse to Sogakope and sales are made by head and not by weight. In spite of inflation in the economy between 1954–64 the prices paid in 1964 were no different from those in 1954, i.e. between £15 to £20 for a bullock and £25 for a heifer.

Cattle bought in this area are taken across the river at either Sogakope or Volo and then sent to markets at Ho, Akuse, Dodowa, Accra and Ada for resale to butchers, where they may fetch up to £45. Blair found that one reason for the low price of cattle was the almost complete lack of competition between dealers, who bought in a buyers' market. There were indications that butchers and itinerant dealers operated in a way intended to keep prices below what Blair called 'reasonable and just'. To remedy this, proposals were made for the establishment of a central livestock market at Sogakope, giving minimum guaranteed prices supported by Government. No such market has yet been established.

White, describing cattle on the Accra Plains in 1953–4 (White, 1954), reported them to be kept for prestige and not for economic purposes. Blair, in 1963, disagreed with this claiming, 'It is often stated that some people who own cattle in Ghana do so principally for reasons of prestige and that they have little or no commercial interest in their herds. Many contacts and conversations with cattle owners do not support this statement'. Little support for prestige motives of ownership in the Lower Volta were found in this study. Many people were, in fact, reluctant to admit to cattle ownership and when they did, often gave misleading information on the location and number of cattle owned.

Nor did people buy cattle in order to resell them at a higher price later; in the absence of seasonal or annual price variation this would in any case have been difficult. From this it has sometimes been concluded that cattle are not kept from economic motives. But that ignores the fact that, in any livestock industry, there is money to be made by letting ones beasts multiply yet keeping numbers constant by either selling the progenitors or their progeny. Assuming a mortality of one calf in three, and allowing one calf in three to be given to the herdsman in payment for his services, a capital growth of at least 20% per annum could be achieved.

Cattle owners are from both sexes and all walks of life: traders, weavers, fishermen, farmers, clerks, civil servants. Reasons given for ownership were mainly that cattle provided quick sources of ready cash. They were sold whenever a sudden emergency occurred which required cash, e.g. funerals, education, debt repayments, or to make a loan. A number of owners sold cattle to buy roofing materials or cement for building. Very rarely were cattle sold to purchase consumer goods, except food and drink for funeral occasions and wake keeping.

As a general rule it was found that cattle were not purchased as an income-earning asset but as a form of security for the future, an investment capable of some capital growth through reproduction but principally as a store of value. They were purchased secretly and kept in a kraal some distance away.

The advantages of investing in cattle in this way are:—

1. It is possible to keep the investment secret from relatives and others.
2. It assures anonymity of ownership.
3. The owner has no direct personal management problems. Though kraals may be very badly managed and many cattle die from poor husbandry and neglect, the owner accepts this as he is only able to visit his cattle occasionally and is probably not in a position to administer a better form of management, even if he knew how to

4. Cattle provide a natural capital growth through progeny.
5. They form a highly liquid investment providing cash for emergencies, such as litigations, funeral expenses, educational fees.
6. Even though the selling price of cattle has not changed much since 1954, investment in cattle has, provided progeny have survived, proved a better hedge against inflation than either bank or post office savings over the last ten years.
7. Cattle owners feel their investment is safe, it is not subject to tax (though a tax of 1/- per head was due it could not be enforced for administrative reasons), and it does not suffer any government interference.

In spite of the low level of husbandry and poor cattle prices, no other investment available offers such attractive terms. Money spent on cattle can be considered a rational use of funds in this illiterate society. Any new capital or technological input into agriculture will have to compete with the advantages which cattle investment offers.

During the Battor survey, records were taken of the number of livestock owned by each household though there was some reluctance to divulge this information. In 1954 eleven households owned a total of over 300 head of cattle, one household owning 100 heads of cattle, two others owning over 50 cattle, and the remainder owning numbers varying from four to 25 head of cattle. It was estimated that some 30 cattle which belonged to people of Battor village were sold in 1954 at an average of £20 per head, bringing an income of about £600 into Battor. By 1964 the ownership of cattle by Battor inhabitants had increased considerably to almost four times the 1954 level though no evidence of any increase in cattle sales was found. However, later between 1965–7 some 250 cattle were sold, mostly to provide funds for house building. This was a period of exceptional building activity, as will be described later, and it appears that sales of cattle were made to provide funds for competitive prestige expenditure on buildings, which took place after 1965.

6 Changes in Trading Activities in the Lower Volta in 1954-64

The limited contact of the Lower Volta with outside markets in 1954 was reflected in its low level of trading activities. As representative of the few larger markets in this area, the market at Aveyime was studied in detail. Many villages had smaller daily markets in which day-to-day surpluses of locally-produced crops were sold. Such a market would vary from three to twenty traders depending on season and size of village and its importance as a social and economic centre. Thus Battor, which had a population of some 700 in 1954, had a daily market of up to 20 women who were most active when there were large gatherings of visitors in the village for festivals and funerals. In such markets there would also be regular visiting fish traders. Fresh meat, usually pork and beef, were hawked by Hausa or Fulani traders from village to village, though not with any regularity. About six Hausa traders peddled haberdashery and fancy goods from village to village in the Lower Volta on a regular routine, though only two visited Battor regularly. One or two women from large markets peddled imported cloth and headscarves round small villages. Few villages on the Lower Volta had stores or shops. On average, a village of 500 to 1000 would support from three to five small stores.

The main means of communication in 1954 was the river, a launch owned by the United African Company plying the river from Ada to Akuse, travelling up and down three times a week. This had ceased by 1964. Three or four sailing barges plied this stretch, taking cargoes of sweet potato, groundnuts and cassava to the road junction at Tefle ferry and to the markets at Ada and Akuse. Over shorter distances canoes of varying sizes carried staple foods to markets along the river and small swift craft could occasionally be seen travelling downstream with cargoes of illicit gin.

Until the improvement of the Battor-Sege track, the river was the only means of getting produce to and from markets outside the area. The main market for goods was Akuse, and here products from the Lower Volta were exchanged for products from the forest. Ada, which is outside the area of this survey, had a market mostly concerned with the export of salt from the nearby lagoon and sea fish, but also it was a centre for the exchange of forest products brought via the Accra market or down the river from Akuse for the onions and fish produced in the Keta peninsula, to which there was constant river traffic. Adidome did not have a very important market in 1954. It was supplied mainly by river transport and served as an entrepot between Keta and the forest areas, goods to the latter travelling on to Akuse mainly by sailing barge or canoe. Aveyime provided the only market which was almost exclusively concerned with produce of the Lower Volta. In 1954 a detailed study was made of this market once per month from May to September. Records were made of the quanity of each item of produce and sources and destinations of produce traded. Daily records were taken of the small market in Battor over the same period and, in each of the stores in Battor, monthly stock-taking and records of supplies received over a period of five months were taken. This enabled estimates of turnover and profits to be made.

i. *The Market at Aveyime in 1954*

Aveyime market served as a collecting centre for produce from a radius of some 8–10 miles. Its importance was due mainly to its location at the centre of the riparian communities of the Lower Volta, its easy access to the river, its location on a track, later improved to become a road, its size and facilities for lorry parking.

From three to ten lorries with an average of six per day visited the market during May to September. The main import by lorry was fish from the coast, especially from Ada, Accra and Prampram but this was largely a seasonal import during August and September and reflected the high seasonal landings of *sardinella*. Much of this was sold wholesale in Aveyime to be retailed later over many months. Pigs and salt came from Ada, onions from Keta. Lorries took away local produce, especially groundnuts, cassava, sweet potato and some vegetables. These were bought by collecting traders for wholesaling, mainly in Accra.

Trade in Aveyime was seasonal, the market diminishing greatly in size during rain and flood seasons. Maximum stocks of produce brought into market from other areas per market day between May to September were 108 baskets of sea fish, 48 pigs, 10 baskets of salt. Maximum stocks of local produce brought into market for export from the area per day during the same period were 218 baskets of groundnuts, 113 bags dried cassava, 95 bags sweet potato, 69 baskets of palm nuts. Much was brought to market by canoe and on one market day 150 incoming canoes were recorded.

In 1954, Aveyime was essentially a market for the sale of local produce by farmers to collecting traders. Small quantities of goods coming into market from other places (apart from fish which was the main protein food) were a function of low standards of living, lack of variety in the diet and the small amounts of cash available. It must be noted also that no imported cloths, headscarves, or any items of wearing apparel were available regularly for sale in the market. One trader occasionally visited the market to sell such goods. One or two Hausa traders sold haberdashery and small household goods like knives and mirrors but no other household goods were for sale.

During the course of the 1954 survey the road between Sege and Aveyime was improved which led to an immediate increase in lorries visiting the market. The growth of Aveyime market after this was undoubtedly associated with further improvements of the road and, by 1964 it had become the main market on the south side of the river, surpassing Akuse and having a turnover some four times the 1954 level.

ii. *Trade in Battor in 1954*

(a) MARKET TRADE

As a contrast to Aveyime, market trade in Battor was mostly concerned with retail sales of local produce, providing supplies for households which, for various reasons, had not been able to harvest their own food supplies, or who wished to purchase foodstuffs such as vegetables, which they did not grow themselves. Traders also provided fish and occasionally meat. The market was held daily in the centre of the village. Between 12–20 traders were present throughout the day and altogether 24 Battor women engaged in market trade, some of them offering a variety of goods for sale. Nine attended market on only one day per week. Only seven were regular daily attenders. With the exception of the latter, all had other occupations, notably diving for clams and farming. Only half the traders gave credit. Bad debts were rare. Profits per trader varied from £2 to £5 per month with an average of about £3 on a turnover of from £10 to £15. i.e. £120–£180 per annum. Many women sold produce from their own farms but expected to make up to 30% profit on goods they bought for resale.

Not all traders in the market were Battor women. Women from nearby hamlets came to sell their harvested crops and creek and river fish. Occasionally, itinerant women traders from Accra, Aveyime and Ada brought headscarves and cloths to market. Two itinerant Hausa men occasionally brought haberdashery, fancy goods, patent medicines and talcum powder. The two most important goods for sale were *kenkey* (fermented corn) and fish which together provided a prepared meal. Bread brought by launch from Ada did not appear for sale in Battor until towards the end of the 1954 survey. The total volume of turnover in the market was about £300 per month, and this was considered a typical monthly average. This level of trade was similar to that occurring in about a dozen larger villages on the Lower Volta.

There were no regular markets in hamlets but they were occasionally visited by itinerant meat traders. It was usual to find one woman in each hamlet who kept small stocks of certain less-perishable foodstuffs for reseale, especially smoked or dried fish.

(b) STORE TRADE

By the end of 1954 there were five stores in Battor, all exclusively sold imported goods. Stocks held at any one time varied from £35 to £84 over the period studied and turnover varied from £10–£35. Drink and tobacco accounted for over half total turnover. Half the imported food for sale consisted of canned sardines and pilchards which were convenience foods used mostly by salaried employees but also used on special occasions in the village. The only other imported foods for sale were evaporated milk, cabin biscuits, cube sugar, corned beef, a small quantity of flour and a few tins of margarine. The small scale of trade reflected the low level of income and purchases were small, for example, sugar was sold in cubes, biscuits singly and cigarettes by the stick. Total turnover of all stores averaged £102 per month and over half the sales were made to non-residents of Battor, mostly from hamlets across the river. Purchases made by Battor residents averaged £5 per annum. Stocks, turnover and profits made by each store are recorded in Table 14.

TABLE 14

Stocks, turnover and profits of stores in Battor in 1954

(Figures quoted refer to the averages per month over the period from May to September, 1954)

		A	B*	C	D	E	Total
Stock at cost	(£'s)	84	65	48	43	36	276
Turnover	(£'s)	35	15	12	30	10	102
Profit	(£'s)	7	2.5	3	6.5	2	21
Rate of Profit on turnover per cent		20	17	25	22	20	20

* Commenced business during survey.

On the basis of records of sales in the market and stores it was possible to summarise the total volume of trade undertaken in Battor in 1954 as follows:

Trade in Stores	Turnover per annum (one half sold to Battor) inhabitants	£1200 approx.
Trade in market	Turnover per annum	£3600 approx.
Total trade per annum		£4800 approx.

Sales made to Battor households totalled £3000 per annum, equivalent to £27 per household. In addition, goods worth an average of £34 per household were purchased from sources outside Battor thus making total cash purchases £61 per annum per household. This amount includes purchases from Aveyime market and the cost of palm wine and gin bought from nearby hamlets.

iii. *The growth of markets, 1954–1967*

Many changes took place in trade and marketing between 1954–67. The markets of the Lower Volta had been transformed. In 1964 there were four very active markets at Aveyime, Akuse, Adidome and Sogakope.

(a) AVEYIME

Aveyime market had increased four-fold in size (see Table 15), following the construction of a new market place, with facilities for lorry parking, the construction of the road from Sege, which enabled traffic to move in all weathers, and to the great increase in agricultural production which followed these infrastructure improvements. A comparison of the goods for sale in 1954 and 1967, given in Table 16, details its growth. The most notable change in Aveyime market in 1964, apart from its increased size, was the great diversity in goods offered for sale. The market had changed from its 1954 characteristic as a market mainly concerned with the collection of local produce and clams from producers in the vicinity and the sale of these to visiting wholesale buyers from large urban centre, to a market which, in addition, was used for the retail sale of a large volume of imported goods to people living in the vicinity. It had thus become a market with a two-way traffic in goods for sale. The most outstanding item brought into the area for local sale was cloth and this, and other clothing, forms the largest item of household expenditure after food. The presence in the market in 1964 of seamstresses, tailors and a shoemaker bears out the increased importance of clothing as an item of household expenditure.

Another change in the market was in the amount of trade carried on at the periphery of the market in a manner described by Miracle in the Congo as 'extra market-place

TABLE 15

Comparative size of Aveyime market, 1954 and 1964*

	1954	1964
Market Frequency	Seasonal, twice weekly.	Year round, twice weekly.
Goods for sale	Almost exclusively local produce, fish and clams	A wide Assortment of local produce and impoted goods, fish and clams.
Volume of local produce brought to market on average day. Index 1954 = 100.	100	403
Number of lorries visiting market per market day.	3–10. None during rainy season	40–50 lorries.
Total number of sellers per day	50–700	270–850
Average number of sellers	180	500

* Data for 1954 relates to the average for main season. At other times the market was depleted owing to its inaccessibility due to flooding of the road. Date for 1964 relates to the average for the year.

sales' (Miracle, 1962, p. 710). This was the trade in prepared and convenience foods and drink. Some of these items were provided by chop bars which sold a variety of imported goods and drinks at all times but which only provided cooked foods during market days. In addition there were itinerant women traders who went from market to market selling cooked foods which were prepared on the spot. The provision of a service which provides cooked meals is an indication of the length of time spent by individual buyers and sellers in the market and in travelling to and from the market and is evidence of the wide area which this market serves.

The range of local foodstuffs appearing in the market had greatly increased since 1954 and this was partly due to an improvement in diet, particularly in the consumption of a wider variety of fruit and vegetables, but partly also to the

TABLE 16

Goods for sale in Aveyime market, 1954 and 1964

1. Local foodstuffs	29 items	43 items
2. Imported foods	None	10 main items, 4 Traders
3. Other imported goods	None, except a) one cloth trader occasionally b) 1–2 house traders selling haberdashery.	4–6 traders selling imported household goods. 40–50 cloth traders, 8 Hausa traders selling haberdashery, 3 sellers of cooked meats.
4. Locally manufactured goods	None except small quantities of shea butter and soap.	10 items
5. Businesses and Crafts conducted within market or on its periphiry.	*Craftsmen* 1 blacksmith 3 tailors 1 seamstress	*Craftsmen* 5 blacksmiths 3 tailors 2 seamstresses 4 goldsmiths 3 carpenters 1 shoemaker 1 fitter
	Other businesses 1 letter writer 2 chop bars 3 licensed bars 1 stationery stall	*Other businesses* 1 letter writer 3 chop bars 5 licensed bars 5 corn mills 2 kerosene/petrol sellers. 1 petrol seller

increased demand for staples not grown in the area, a demand which met the needs of an immigrant population of wage employees from areas outside the region. The large number of lorries visiting the market in 1964 required the support of a petrol seller and a fitter and these operated on the periphery of the market. The increase in locally manufactured goods consisted of both consumer and producer goods, for instance simple agricultural tools, fishing gear, cooking pots, baskets, wooden spoons, calabashes, mats, string and twine.

Most traders in the market were full time traders by occupation. Those who were visting the market from outside the area were generally either collecting buyers of produce or itinerant traders who moved from market to market in a regular routine. Amongst those traders who lived in the area there was evidence of specialisation which did not exist in 1954. For instance there were a few local traders who specialised in buying fruit and vegetables from distant areas and who sold in this and other markets in the area. There were many more local traders in local produce who had bought direct from producers to sell to collecting traders, than existed in 1954. This was particularly in evidence in the sale of clams and though this trend had been noted in the 1954 study it had, by 1964, become a more specialised occupation for about one fifth of the sellers of clams in the market. It was evident that the purchase of produce from farmers and fishermen was becoming a specialised occupation for a small number of local people, whereas in 1954 the sale of own-produce was generally undertaken by a member of the producing household.

In 1964 the market had become the centre of a number of diverse trades and small industries e.g. goldsmithing, foundry work, corn mills, tailors, seamstresses, carpenters, shoemakers, letter writers. Craftsmen and traders involved in these occupations may at first be itinerant from market to market as far as their capital equipment allows them to be mobile, but when demand is sufficient they establish themselves in small stores or shacks on the periphery of the market and become settled. This is especially the case with seamstresses, tailors and shoemakers. Letter writers may develop a trade in stationery.

(b) AKUSE

In 1954, Akuse was very important as a trading centre (Government Statistician, Accra, 1954) since it was near the river terminal of the launch which plied the Lower Volta from Ada three times a week and also to the main trans-Volta ferry which, before the bridge was constructed over the Volta a few miles further north, provided the major link between south and west of Ghana and regions to the east of the Volta including what was then British Togoland. The market thus provided an important collecting and distributing centre for produce from all regions of Ghana. It also had a thriving trade in imported goods, having branches of four large expatriate-owned stores, seven African-owned stores, eleven other small businesses, mainly carpenters, seamstresses and tailors and a market trade which included a range of imported goods, especially textiles, hardware and a small quantity of imported food. The turnover of small African-owned stores was in the region of £240 to £400 per annum probably over half of this being accounted for by drinks, tobacco and cigarettes.

After the construction of the bridge over the Volta a few miles north of Akuse, most traffic passed directly across the river and trade in the town fell considerably. By 1964 the expatriate-owned stores and businesses were heavily depleted, the market was oriented towards a much more highly localised custom but even so, it contained a much wider assortment of goods than in 1954. Records of all goods entering and leaving the market were made in July 1964 which corresponded to the month in 1954 when similar records were taken by the Office of the Government Statistician. New items of imported goods which appeared for sale in 1964 including large quantities of cement, iron sheets, iron rods, towels and shoes, reflected the improvement in rural housing and living standards.

(c) ADIDOME

By 1964 Adidome had adopted a much more urban character than any other village on the Lower Volta. In 1954 it had 34 small business and trading establishments. Most trade in imported goods was undertaken through branches of two large expatriate companies. Five small African-owned enterprises also handled imported goods and survived the competition of the expatriate firms by selling in small quantities and giving credit.

By 1964 there were 15 stores in Adidome, the two previously owned by expatriate firms had changed to Ghanaian hands. There was a wide range in value and variety of stocks held, varying from the £5000 and £3000 of the two expatriate owned business, down to the smallest with stocks less than £100. Stocks in hand reflected a more sophisticated demand for imported goods than elsewhere on the Lower Volta and included, for example, imported plastic toys, a wide range of toothpastes, women's underwear, ladies blouses (imported) and a range of imported kitchen utensils. The number of business and trading establishments in Adidome increased to 93 by 1964 comprising the following: 12 transport undertakings, 10 tailors, 8 bread bakers (one in 1954) 7 cornmillers, 5 seamstresses, 4 building contractors, 8 chop bars, 3 goldsmiths, 2 gin distillers, 3 barbers, 15 general stores, 14 weavers.

Adidome market in 1964 had an assortment of goods similar to that at Aveyime but, in addition, it had a large trade in local pots made in Vume across the river. The modal number of sellers in 1964 was 100 per market day, details of which are given in Table 17. The volume of trade carried on in the market had increased fourfold over 1954.

(d) SOGAKOPE

Sogakope market had developed since 1954 when the only trade undertaken was by a few traders selling prepared goods to ferry passengers. By 1964 it had developed into a large market as both a distributing and collecting centre. Some of its trade, notably in groundnuts, clams and sea fish was highly seasonal but it had a fairly regular trade in salt, charcoal, vegetables, cassava and cassava products and oils, pots and imported goods, especially textiles, certain inexpensive household goods and certain canned foods. The modal number of traders present in the market in 1964 was 250 per market day. Trade in local produce predominated in Sogakope and Adidome and main items handled and number of traders involved are given in Table 17.

(e) BATTOR

By 1964 the market at Battor had practically disappeared from the centre of the village. In 1954 there had been up to 20 traders in the market selling 13 different food products.

72   THE CHANGING ECONOMY OF THE LOWER VOLTA

TABLE 17

*Market trade in Adidome and Sogakope, 1964,
main items of produce only*

	Usual number of traders	
Produce in market	Adidome	Sogakope
Clams—Highly seasonal changes	Up to 36	Up to 19
Kokonte (dried cassava)— seasonal changes	25	30—66
Fresh cassava	10—22	5—9
Gari (grated dried cassava)	10—14	4—7
Okro	10—13	7—9
Groundnuts—high seasonal, none present out of season	37 at peak	10 at peak
Pepper	17—30	28
Maize	10—20	30
Cassava dough	25	16
Creek and river fish	12	8—25
Charcoal	15	15
Salt	20	7—17
Tomatoes	20	20
Palm Kernels	7	7
Cooking Oil	16	16
Sea fish—smoked, high seasonal peaks	11—51	18—66
Sea fish—dried, seasonal peaks	17	17
Modal Number in Market	100	250

By 1964 this had fallen to only 4—8 traders selling 12 food products. The market had however been re-located on a piece of land adjacent to the hospital and consisted of 20—30 women who attended daily and sold mostly prepared foods, oranges and other fruit mostly to persons visiting the hospital and to school children. Many prepared and convenience foods had been introduced into the market since 1954 e.g. fruit (oranges, bananas), cooked groundnuts, biscuits, and bread. The greatest volume of trade, probably 70%, was to non-residents of Battor. On the basis of random studies, annual turnover in 1964 in the market was estimated to be around £5,000, averaging £100 to £200 per trader.

By 1964 store trade in Battor had increased threefold in value in turnover, though 20% of this could be accounted for by price increases since 1954. The growth in store trading is analysed in Table 18. The sales of imported food and toilet preparations had increased quantitatively fivefold. Household durables and local foods were new items in stock. Purchases of imported drink and tobacco had in fact fallen in quantitative terms by over half, since prices rose over the period and demand was highly price elastic. It must be noted, however, that by far the largest proportion of drink consumed in this area is illicitly locally-distilled gin. Stocks, turnover and profits of stores in 1964 had increased two to three times over 1954 levels. It must be noted that about three-quarters of the sales made through stores in 1964 were sold to Battor inhabitants compared to one half in 1954. Stocks, turnover and profits of stores in 1964 are given in Table 19.

TABLE 18

Turnover of goods in stores in Battor in 1954 and 1964 as percent of total turnover

	1954	1964	Percentage increase in turnover by 1964
Imported foods	17	31	500
Drink and Tobacco	53	29	150
Household Durables	–	3	New item
Medicine	9	7	200
Toilet preparations	5	15	500
Local Food	–	2	New item
Miscellaneous	16	13	
	100	100	
Total in £ for the year	£1224*	£3300	
Average per household per annum in Battor	£5	£22	

*Based on data taken over five months.

The years 1964–67 were very unstable for store trade in Battor; this reflected general inflation over the period and the great increase in prices of imported foods due largely to shortages but also to increases in import duties. At the beginning of 1964 there were four stores in Battor. A small store was opened by a clerk during the year. By the end of 1964 turnover and stock had become seriously depleted and later two stores closed down and others had very low turnovers. Stockes were not replenished as storekeepers were obliged to pay black market prices to wholesalers in Accra and this pushed the retail price out of range of Battor consumers. However, in order to make a comparison of business activity in a fairly normal period of the year, trade in the months May to September are summarised here and this period corresponds to the period recorded for 1954 in Table 18.

TABLE 19

Stocks, turnover and profits of stores in Battor, 1964

(Figures given refer to the averages per month over the period May to September, 1964)

	A	B	C	D	E	TOTAL
Stock at cost (£'s)	154	91	21	11	160	437
Turnover (£'s)	99	64	14	16	100	293
Profit (£'s)	21	16	4	8	21	70
Rate of profit on turnover per cent.	21	25	30	50	21	24

Notes:

1. Little co-operation was forthcoming from storekeeper of store E and figures given here are based on visual observations and stocktaking.
2. Storekeeper D was a clerk who commenced business early in 1964 but who went out of business later that year.
3. Store C had been in operation since 1954. The business had declined owing to old age of the storekeeper and closed down in late 1964.

Though turnover had nearly doubled since 1954, profits had trebled. The only two stores however which showed an exceptional achievement in terms of rate of profit were small stores which had a very small range of stocks consisting mostly of drink, which was still a very profitable line. Both stores however went out of business later in the year. Excluding these from the others, the rate of profit averages

22% compared to 21% in 1954. Only storekeepers A, E, and C had no other employment.

The total volume of trade undertaken in Battor in 1964 was as follows:—

Sales made in market	£5,000
Sales made through stores	£3,300
Total trade	£8,300

Of the above some £4,900 was sold to inhabitants of Battor during the year giving an average per household of about £39 compared to £27 in 1954. It must be noted however that much greater quantities of goods were bought in other places than in 1954, and were brought into Battor by lorry. In 1964 an average of 50 lorries entered Battor per month and there were six regular lorries which plied the route to Accra. This can be compared to one per month in 1954.

Amongst those who have capital resources to purchase initial stocks, there is a certain amount of mobility in and out of store-trading, especially where it is carried on as a subsidiary source of income and employment. This easy mobility arises largely because overheads and capital investment are small. Initially capital must be sufficient to purchase opening stocks but these can be small. Rentals are minimal and in some cases the store is formed from a converted room in the house. The mobility of resources and persons in and out of store trade is probably characteristic of an economy in transition when individuals are seeking new employment opportunities and are limited by the alternatives offered in the society.

iv. *Trends in the changes in marketing and trade*

On the basis of this study the following conclusions on changes in marketing in the Lower Volta during the period of economic growth can be made.

i. Rural economic growth has been accompanied by the growing importance of the market. The market is not only used for collection and distribution of local produce but also for retail trade of a wide range of imported goods such as cloth, clothes, household goods, medicines, imported foods and so on. New items which appear for sale in rural areas appear first in the market and, only when there is an established demand, does entrepreunership move to the establishment of stores. The market is the centre of a number of diverse trades and small industries, e.g. goldsmithing, foundries, corn mills, tailors, seamstresses, carpenters, shoemakers, letter writers. Craftsmen and traders involved in these occupations may be itinerant from market to market as far as their capital equipment allows them to be mobile, but when demand is sufficient they become settled in small stores or shacks on the periphery of the market, e.g. seamstresses, shoemakers, letter writers.

ii. There is a wider range of imported goods for sale in markets than local foodstuffs which are grown in other areas. This is partly a function of the system of distribution. Collecting traders come to market from distant places to buy large quantities of one product but do not bring into the market produce from other areas. Produce from other areas is brought into market by local traders who travel away to buy a variety of produce from distant markets. As there are few such people prices tend to be high. The relatively small amount of local foodstuffs for retail sale in the market reflects the continuing high level of subsistence production.

Retail demands for local produce not grown in the area arise chiefly from immigrants to the area, e.g. teachers, clerks, etc. who find that unless they undertake subsistence farming, the cost of food in the country is often higher than in towns where they are able to get a wider range of produce at more competitive prices.

However, in rural areas those foodstuffs which are produced in the area are sometimes also scarce. The reason for this is that whilst there may be a good wholesale market in the rural area, so that visiting, collecting traders have easy access to supplies direct from the farm, there is not much demand at a retail level, especially in the small markets, and locally-produced foods are sometimes difficult to obtain and prices are high.

iii. This study revealed much greater elasticity in the supply of marketing services in wholesale trade in local produce than in retail trade in foodstuffs not grown in the locality

(Lawson, 1971). The markets of the Lower Volta confirm that the movement of food in Ghana is largely a movement of cash crops from rural areas direct to the urban centres and there is less interchange between rural areas of the specialised crops which they grow. Exceptions to this are the non-carbohydrate staples, e.g. fish, salt, oils. However, the interchange in other foods between rural areas is increasing with the greater inflow of people from different regions, where dietary patterns are different and this is slowly bringing a greater diversity of local foodstuffs into rural markets.

It must be noted, however, that rural economic growth leads to a flow of cash income which becomes available for nonfood expenditure. In the Lower Volta the most notable increase in retail trade was in sale of cloths and imported household durables and marketing services in these products has always been highly elastic in supply. The reasons for this are that such products are easily portable from one market to another, they do not deteriorate, they can be stored and are highly price elastic.

iv. At a rural level, capital moves in and out of small store trading with easy mobility. Some stores may only open for a season and the high mortality rate of small businesses is not necessarily associated with failure but with the need for flexibility and diversity in sources of employment and income at this stage of growth. Small storekeeping does not provide an adequate household income for more than probably two stores in a village of 700 and other stores are usually only open for business at times which fit into the owner's other occupations. Business depends very much on trade in imported foods and if these are scarce and a black market price rules (as occurred in 1965/6) then business falls off sharply owing to the high price elasticity of demand.

v. Growth in size of markets is partly a function of increased accessibility of markets due to improvements of roads and transport facilities and these lead to an icrease in the quantity of foodstuffs brought to market. It could be argued that a large marketable surplus is a pre-condition for road and market construction but in Ghana many rural roads have been built for a variety of non-economic reasons, e.g. national prestige, defence, internal politics, etc. The Lower

Volta has expanded its economy through the improvement of roads made for reasons not initially associated with an increase in traditional farming, (two Ministers of Finance lived in this region) and the effect of road improvement has been to increase the size and scope of markets and the volume of local produce passing through them, resulting from an increase in marketable surpluses.

7 Changes in Income and Wealth in 1954-64

By 1964 new large villages had developed in the Lower Volta, new roads had been constructed, schools, clinics, hospitals had opened. In Asuchare district a start had been made by the government to develop cane sugar plantations to provide the nearby sugar refinery. In the Adidome area a large state farm under Soviet management was starting to introduce large-scale farming of rice and maize using labour from the State Farms organisation with little local farm labour. In the Aveyime area the Ministry of Agriculture was carrying out field trials in cropping vegetables using labour from outside the area. There were also plans for a state-owned tannery at Aveyime using Czechoslovak machinery and management. All these were state-introduced schemes. None had reference to needs of local farmers who were remote bystanders in these developments, which were beyond their technical knowledge and managerial ability. Nearly all of these state schemes had failed by 1967, some being halted with the coup in 1966. None, except co-operative farming of sugar, had any lasting effect on peasant farmers and traditional agricultural practices noticed in 1954 had remained unchanged in 1967.

However the influx into the Lower Volta of large amounts of state capital and hundreds of wage employed people to work on these state-managed schemes did have a favourable effect on the local economy. Roads were improved and subsequently markets increased in both size and volume of trade. Housing provided for the 'strangers' was far superior to that of the indigenous population, demonstrating new standards to them. The demand for imported food increased bringing

80 THE CHANGING ECONOMY OF THE LOWER VOLTA

growth in store trading. There was an immediate market for cash crops. These were all visible changes. However more profound and permanent change to the economy was brought out by the influence of 'strangers' on the traditional structure, customs and attitudes of riparian communities. The demonstration effect of having large numbers of 'strangers' in their midst not only exposed them to new levels of demand and higher standards of living but also to new social structures and new status symbols and gave opportunities for deviance from static traditions.

Before returning to discuss this in more detail, the 1964 situation must be analysed. Immediately before 1964 there had been a serious flood in the Lower Volta. In early 1964 the dam was closed, the Lake began to build up and 1963 was the last year in which the river flooded. The study, in 1964, of the riparian community thus represented the last year in which the condition of the river, riparian land, creeks and streams were at all comparable with conditions in 1954. The study continued to 1967, and between 1964–67 still further change became apparent in the economy. This was triggered off by two events, first the exceptional floods of 1963 had destroyed some of the mud-constructed houses by the river and there was an immediate need to rebuild. Secondly, the filling of the Lake in these years led to the development of a prolific fishery which attracted large numbers of fishermen from the Lower Volta and who, as a result, were able to bring increased incomes back to their downstream villages.

These two events led, in 1965–7, to an enormous house-building boom. Capital involved in this however could not be accounted for by the recent increased incomes from fishing alone and it was obvious that a large amount of savings had been made in the economy over the years between 1954 and 1964. These savings concealed a rate of growth in the economy which was not made apparent by studies of standards of consumption and inventories of apparent possessions. There had, however, been considerable improvements in both of these and in aggregate incomes, between 1954 and 1964, as demonstrated in Tables 20, 21 and 22.

Two date lines will be considered, first, 1964, when, on

TABLE 20

Structure of aggregate income for Battor, including value of subsistence production

1954 and 1964 in £'s sterling at current prices

Source of Income	1954	1964
	£	£
Farming (including oil palms and cattle)	4,587	12,700
Fishing	2,350	8,314 *
Clam Diving	1,000	2,604 *
Self-employed in crafts	1,100	2,000
Trading and Stores	1,000	2,396
Salaries and wages	3,800	6,550
	13.837	34,564
Average income per household (144 in 1954 and 136 in 1964)	96	254
Average income per capita	20	50
Average income per capita *excluding* windfall receipts from clams and fish		45

* Estimated exceptional income due to changes in conditions of the river in 1964 clams—£1050, fish—£3,000.

Note: The figures in Table 20 are at current prices. It must be noted that the retail price index rose to 185 in 1964 (1954 = 100). Taking this into account real incomes probably rose by some 22% between 1954 and 1964, representing an average annual growth rate of 2% in real terms or 6% at current prices.

the basis of levels of consumption there appeared to have been some growth over the 1954 level, and 1967 when the housing boom gave ample, easily visible, evidence that savings which had been accumulated had been spent and considerable growth had taken place since 1954. It was evident that between 1954—64 the rate of growth in consumption expenditure did not keep pace with the rate of growth in income. The level of consumption was kept down by traditional sanctions and savings were thus immobilised because of social restraints and were not diverted into visibly productive investment because they had to be kept secret. This secrecy was broken with the housebuilding boom which was triggered off by an obvious and well-known increase in

82   THE CHANGING ECONOMY OF THE LOWER VOLTA

income from lake fishing, which could not be concealed. Much money from this source was then spent on prestigious house construction. This served to spur on others who had built up secret hoards over the previous years, to bring their concealed savings into the open and they too entered the housebuilding boom in a somewhat competitive spirit. It should be noted that such houses had no effective rental value since there was no demand for rented accommodation. Thus, between 1965–67 newly mobilised savings were not invested for productive purposes but for reasons of personal and family prestige, following an accepted show of achievement. The loss of such funds to more productive investment operates as a constraint to economic growth.

The changes which took place in income and wealth in Battor between 1954, 1964 and 1967 are shown in Tables 20, 22 and 23.

TABLE 21

Monthly household income levels in Battor.
1954 and 1964, in £'s sterling at current prices

Income group £	1954 * £	1964 ** £
0– 2.49	13	–
2.5– 4.99	71	2
5.0– 7.49	34	18
7.5– 9.99	23	32
10.0–12.49	5	46
12.5–14.99	–	23
15.0–17.49	–	9
17.5–and over	–	6
Average per annum	96	254

* 1954 figures are based on an expenditure survey of 57 households over four months. A cross check on these figures was provided by aggregating income from all sources over the year and on this basis it seemed reasonable to assume that for nearly all households there was no net savings and income equalled expenditure. There were however probably some five or six exceptions to this for some savings had been diverted into cattle, mostly by seine net owners.
** 1964 figures are based on aggregating household incomes from all sources using a 50% sample of all households, and cross checking with data on value of fish, farm and clam production.

TABLE 22

*Aggregate ownership of goods and property in
Battor, 1954 and 1967 at 1966 prices in Ghana £'s**

		1954 £G	1967 £G
I. Producer Goods:			
1 Fishing	Canoes	540	696
	Nets, traps etc.	1560	2228
2. Farming	Hoes	97	100
	Cutlasses	42	44
3. Guns	(Partly prestigious and for ceremonies)	252	270
		2491	3338
II. Farm Animals:			
1. Cattle	(Cattle worth probably £5000 sold between 1964–67 to provide funds for investment in housing	6180	17825
	Chickens	155	310
	Pigs (not restocked after all had died of disease)	290	—
	Goats	392	897
	Sheep	1463	1002
	Other	—	59
		8480'	20093
III. Buildings:			
Houses (completed and under construction)		5850	40430
IV. Household Goods:			
Bedding and household durables and furniture		576	13102
Clothing		650	14632
		1226	27734
V. Gold Ornaments:		Not recorded	1029
Total		18447	92624
VI. Average per household excluding the three highest in 1964, and excluding gold ornaments. in 1954.		128	515

TABLE 23

Numbers and values of house buildings in Battor, 1954 and 1967 at 1967 prices in £'s sterling *

Type of House	1954		1967	
	No.	Total Value	No.	Total Value
		£		£
Swish with thatch @ £20 average 90	90	1800	39	780
Swish with iron roof @ £50 average	51	2550	36	1800
Swish with iron roof (larger house), £100 average	–	–	20	2000
Storey house, swish with iron roof, £500 average	3	1500	–	–
Concrete block house with iron roof				
Average value £350			11	3850
Average value £550			16	8800
Average value £900			10	9000
Storey houses **			4	14200
	144	5850	136	40430
Average value per house		40		300
Average value of swish houses		40		46
Average value of concrete houses				874

* Each house was valued separately on basis of cost of materials and labour costs, excluding value of unpaid labour. Houses in 1954 valued at 1967 prices before devaluation. There were four concrete block houses in 1964.
** Includes large house built by lorry driver.

Note to Table 22: 1967 data are based on inventory of 50 per cent of households and cost evaluations of all housebuilding. 1954 data are based on 100 per cent inventory with the exception of IV, Household Goods, which was based on a 10 per cent sample. There were 144 households in 1954 and 136 in 1967

* Prices are given at 1966 levels since, in 1967, the Ghana £ was devalued. Hitherto £G1 = £1 sterling.

TABLE 24

Main sources of earnings of funds used for investment in housebuilding in Battor and Adidome between 1964 and 1967 *

Main Source of funds		Houses in Battor	Houses in Adidome
Primary Production			
Cattle farming		4	5
Food crop farming		1	—
Coffee farming	) out of the	1	—
Cocoa farming	) area	2	1
Fishing		14	9
		22	15
Manufacturing			
Distilling Gin		1	2
Tailoring		1	—
Carpentry		1	2
		3	4
Trade and Transport			
Storekeeping		1	3
Petty trade in	(a) fish and clams	4	3
	(b) food	1	4
	(c) other	1	4
Lorry ownership		1	3
		8	17
Employment			
Unskilled labour		2	—
Clerks		2	6
		4	6
Total number of houses		37	42
Total value as in 1967		£31,500	£42,300
Average value of investment per house		£854	£1,007

1. This excludes investment in housebuilding made by Members of Parliament (two in Adidome, one in Battor) and the houses constructed for the District Commissioners and the church missions and hospitals.
2. There were in addition 27 other new houses either completed or under construction in Adidome about which no information of sources of investment could be obtained, largely on account of absence of owners.
3. The employments listed here are the original sources of earnings. Savings were mostly either kept in cash or invested in cattle.

TABLE 25

Distribution of total value of assets of households*
taking all households in Battor in 1954 and 1967

Value of household assets in £'s sterling	Number of households 1954	1967
£		
0– 249	110	63
250– 499	27	38
500– 749	3	10
750– 999	2	8
1000–1249	2	7
1250–and over **	–	10
Total number of households	144	136

* Assets include producer goods, capital goods, household durables, property and buildings.
** Of the last group, three had high levels of ownership: e.g. £2,590, £8,300 and £11,600 in 1967.

TABLE 26

Number of items of specific durable household goods owned in Battor in 1954 and 1967 *

	1954	1967
Total number of households	144	136
Durable goods in Battor		
Gramophones	5	–
Radios	–	20
Bicycles	11	16
Clocks and watches	6	25
Sewing machines	6	18
Guns	42	45
Mosquito nets	50	109

* Data for 1954 and 1967 given in Tables 25, 26 were based on complete inventories made in each household by individual interviews.

Aggregate village income in Battor in 1964 increased to 250% over 1954 levels. It would be erroneous however to consider increased income as a measure of increased labour productivity without considering price changes. In fact local foodstuff prices rose 85% between 1954–64. In agriculture there was a slight increase in labour productivity but most of the increase in earnings arose because of the larger numbers of people involved in farming, and the rise in local foodstuff prices. Fishing incomes increased considerably in 1964 but this cannot be taken as indicating a permanent increase in incomes since the earnings from fishing are very volatile from year to year and 1964 was exceptional. Aggregate incomes from salaries and wages rose, partly because increased labour was employed but also because the introduction in July 1960 of minimum statutory wage legislation caused wages for unskilled labour to increase by some 45% and other wages and salaries to rise also but by lesser proportions.

Aggregate income, including the value of food and fish used for domestic consumption, rose from £96 in 1954 to £254 per household in 1964, (see Table 21) or, on a per capita basis, from £20 to £50. These figures may be compared with the per capita income of £92, estimated from the 1964 Gross Domestic Product. There was no Gross Domestic Product data for 1954, but average incomes of the people of the Lower Volta were undoubtedly below national average but probably similar to the large proportion of people living in rural Ghana.

Allowing for exceptional earnings in 1964 from fishing and clam diving, which together amount to £4,000, the growth in aggregate incomes at current prices between 1954—64 represents a growth rate of about 6% per annum.

However, in view of inflation which took place between these years, it is not possible to say accurately what this represents in real terms, though an average real growth rate of 2% can be estimated. Assuming this rate of growth and taking into account an inflation by 1964 of 85% over a base of 1954=100*, it seems likely that total aggregate incomes arising in Battor from sources already listed and including the value of production for household consumption, would total, over the ten year period, at least £200,000.

In 1954 a significant net surplus of annual income over annual expenditure occurred in probably only some five to six households. By 1964 the number of households making net annual savings had greatly increased and a high marginal

* Calculated from consumer price data, Central Bureau of Statistics, Accra.

propensity to save seemed evident. The standard of living and ownership of domestic durables had however also considerably improved. Detailed evidence of these improvements are given in Tables 22 and 26.

Table 22 lists all property, producer goods and household durables owned in the village. On average, households owned items worth £680, equal to 2.5 years' household income. However there was a great difference between wealthy and poor households as shown in Table 25. Nearly half the households had assets worth less than £250 and this group formed the mode.

In aggregate the value of goods and property owned by Battor inhabitants had increased five-fold between 1954 and 1967. However, in view of inflation a more realistic assessment of the increase in these values is shown in Table 26 which lists the most important items of household durables. The number of mosquito nets had doubled, sewing machines trebled, and clocks and watches increased fourfold. Two other notable items in Table 22 are the increases in values of houses and cattle owned. In 1964 there was some difficulty to get individuals to admit to cattle ownership, as explained earlier, but on finding evidence of ownership from devious sources (e.g. from cattle herdsmen and others), and also by inquiring in 1967 how persons had obtained funds to spend on house building, a high level of cattle ownership was revealed.

The most obvious increase in wealth and ownership was evidenced in the 1965–67 housing boom. Aggregate value of houses in 1964 was estimated at £13,430. The value of each individual house was obtained on the basis of evaluation of cost of materials, mainly cement, sold in standard bags, and scantlings, doors, frames and roofing materials. A further £27,000 was spent on housing between 1965–67. This figure was obtained by regularly recording the increased building activity in the village. In 1954 there were no houses constructed of cement in Battor. In 1964 there were only four. By 1967 there were forty-one. It must be noted that, whilst there were some 14 new houses valued at an average of £900, there were also some very humble houses, thirty-nine having values less than £20.

This sudden increase in spending on housing was so spectacular that a follow-up study was made to find the source of funds which financed this housing boom. Thirty seven persons in Battor and forty two persons in Adidome who had made considerable improvements to their houses were interviewed and results of the findings are given in Table 24. It was found that, in fact, savings had been accumulated from a number of employments over a number of years. Table 24 lists the main original source of income from which savings had been made. Individuals were reluctant to admit fully as to where these savings had been kept but it was evident that much had been invested in cattle. Fishing provided the most important original source of savings, with trade second. Out of those accumulating savings from trade, six in Battor and ten in Adidome were women. No women made savings from clam fishing unless she also engaged in trade in clams.

Apart from the spectacular housing boom and the evolution of a high rural marginal propensity to save which it exposed, another important aspect of rural economic growth which became evident was the widening difference between rich and poor. This was not obvious in this community until after 1964 when the housing boom started. Until then households in the traditional sector had an appearance of a fairly uniform level of wealth and income. Levels of consumption were fairly constant between households and the main deviants from this level were the wage earners and 'strangers'.

Table 23 illustrates the great differences in standards of housing in 1967 between those owning swish built houses and those owning concrete houses. There is, of course, no justification for believing that none of the people living in poorer houses had secret hoards and savings which remained unspent and which they were not yet prepared to display, but the wide range in earnings from fishing and agriculture supported the belief that there were many poor people in this community, as well as a number of wealthier people who could afford to spend substantial sums on housing. Even with recent displays of wealth through prestige housing, there is no indication that other standards of living are changing and it seems likely, as Field has related about cocoa farming villages (Field, 1960, pp. 32–33), that, in spite of the facade of fine houses, money is seldom spent on raising the basic standards of living. If this continues to occur, a fund of savings will again accumulate to await a new round of prestige spending sometime in the future unless better uses can be found for rural savings.

In a fairly contained community like this, where traditional culture still has some constraining influence on consumption spending, accepted prestige spending appears to occur in cycles. These cycles however are probably not regular in periodicity but are probably determined by an exogeneous factor which triggers off a round of spending. It may well be that the lull which follows afterwards, in which there is little visible evidence of an increase in spending or the accumulation of wealth, has led some economists to consider that such communities have limited aspirations. However, whilst it may appear under such conditions that growth takes place in a series of steps and plateaus, the contention here is that growth takes place gradually, savings are accumulated secretly or inconspicuously so that when social conditions allow it, a spree of spending takes place. However no event would trigger off a process of prestige spending unless there were already a large amount of savings available for spending amongst many people in the community, since the display of ostentation by a few would not be acceptable. It should be noted that, in this rural community, funds are rarely borrowed for house building, apart from small amounts on a very short term basis, since house building is an indication of achievement.

PART III

Economic Processes of Change

Ghana is a developing economy which continues to have a high percentage of its population engaged in agriculture in which no structural changes have yet taken place. Much of the rural economy still appears to be entrenched in a traditional Schultzian-type culture (Schultz, 1964, chaps. 1 and 2) and there is little evidence of the appurtenances of economic growth which are so obvious in urban Ghana. In this study of rural change in the Lower Volta it has been possible, however, to quantify certain changes which have taken place. An attempt is now made to understand why these and not others have occurred.

i. *Changes in socio-economic structure*
These can be enumerated as follows:
1. There has been a marked reduction in the time spent on ceremonial activities notably funerals and customary celebrations. The number of days per adult spent at funerals and wake-keeping in 1964 fell to 2 per month from 5 in 1954. In 1954 there was nearly always a funeral in progress and in Battor averaged seven per month, the rites usually taking 5 to 6 days to perform, one taking ten days. By 1964, time spent on funeral rites had fallen to two or three days. The amount of drink consumed at funerals fell from 2% of total household expenditure to 0.5% in 1964 and this represents, allowing for price changes, a halving of the amount consumed. It is not unusual for participants (100–200 persons) in a funeral to consume between them 16 gallons of local gin.

In 1964 there was a noticeable change in the pattern of visiting. Whereas in 1954, funerals and other customs attracted large numbers of visitors, sometimes over 100, by 1964, both the frequency and number of persons visiting the village had diminished. Few funerals had more than 30 or 40 visitors from elsewhere. Male farmers however appeared to spend a lot of time out of the village visiting or travelling and spent an average of 28 days each per annum on 'travelling'. This is, however, higher than the average for the total adult population. A separate study of visits made out of the village by all adults living in Battor, excluding time spent on marketing, was undertaken in 1964. The time spent away by male heads of households (except those going away for fishing) was as much as that spent by male farmers. However, wives, especially second and third wives, spent little time on 'travelling' usually only 4 to 8 days per year. Exceptions to this were traders, who spent much time out of the village and travelled frequently to big towns some distance away, e.g. Accra, Akosombo, Korforidua. Travelling for trade purposes is a relatively new activity. In 1954, Battor traders relied on getting supplies from Aveyime market and only one or two women travelled to more distant markets.

Though no quantitative data were recorded for 1954 the changes in the pattern of visiting since then appeared to be:

(a) Fewer visits to and from local hamlets. This may be associated with the decline in population of small villages and hamlets.
(b) Visiting is frequently undertaken by male heads of households and had increased, especially among farming households.
(c) Few women 'visit' but many more go regularly to Aveyime market. This is associated with the greater amount of farm produce passing through markets. At least one woman per household visited the market once per week, spending the whole day there.
(d) Traders went much further afield than in 1954.
(e) Visits to Accra were much more frequent. Five regular passengers lorries plied between Battor and Accra two or three times per week. In 1954 a lorry came only once per month to Battor.

2. There are indications that a class structure is beginning to develop which is based on wealth and ownership of material goods. This, however, has not yet completely replaced the

traditional tribal and clan structure. Some decline in the status of traditional leaders has however occurred and the culture associated with chiefly institutions is undergoing change. The importance of the position of the chief and the cultural activities surrounding him declined throughout Ghana during the Nkrumah regime. Political organisations introduced by the Convention Peoples Party to replace some functions of the chief however, did not attract, in the rural community, the same amount of traditional festivity or occupy so much time as those concerned with traditional leaders.

Three District Commissioners (political appointments) were stationed in this section of the Lower Volta after 1957, one at Battor. These men brought new status symbols, such as large cars, modern houses, many imported consumer durables (refrigerators, radios, modern kitchen equipment etc.) and though many of the individuals involved in this affluence were discredited after the fall of Nkrumah, they left behind them a new pattern of status and prestige which is not entirely despised and there is now a growing respect and effective demand for prestigous consumer goods The withdrawal of status from traditional rulers gave the opportunity for new status seekers to emerge. This, together with an increasing demand for consumer goods, are considered by some economists to be important preconditions for economic growth.

3. The culturally determined level of subsistence has moved upwards from 1954 levels. This has been due to a number of factors. The most important is the demonstration effect of consumption patterns set by a number of 'strangers' in the society, most of whom were wage and salary earners who were better educated than village people and who had a higher level of consumption. These strangers gradually became integrated into the village. They may be compared to Hoselitz's minority groups which, he claims, play an important contributory role in development (Hoselitz, 1957). In Battor 'strangers' not only introduced a higher level of subsistence but their influence eventually led to a breakdown in rigid conformity to established patterns of consumption.

For example, at the level of consumer durables, teachers

introduced bicycles and gramophones in the 1950's and later transistor radios and cameras, though these were far beyond the resources of people in the traditional sector. They also introduced less expensive consumer goods, such as imported household enamel ware, cups, saucers, drinking glasses, domestic utensils (plastic and metal), imported medicines and certain imported foodstuffs. These were gradually assimilated over a period of ten years into the traditional pattern of consumption. The standard of living however did not, by 1967, demand plastic tablecloths, facial cosmetics, handbags, underwear etc., which were demanded by urban women. Data on the changes in standards of ownership of household durables are given in Table 22.

Another factor which has affected consumption levels is the greater mobility of people to markets and large urban centres. This has occurred largely as a result of improved roads and marketing facilities which has given rural people the opportunity to see a wider shop-window. There has been an increased demand for goods, especially clothing connected with health and education improvements. For example, in 1954 children were mostly naked or half naked but in 1964 nudity was rare. In 1954 very few people, apart from the male head, owned shoes or sandals. In 1964 children had to wear shoes for school, though not all adult females owned either shoes or sandals. There was a large range of baby foods and medicines for sale in the stores and this was partly due to the influence of the hospital and clinic.

New wage employments in the village and a higher level of income from farming led to increased permanent income flows. Some of this eventually went to support a higher level of subsistence but until this occurred a proportion of income was not spent on consumption but was either hoarded or spent on cattle.

4. The instability which accompanies economic growth brought the need to provide for greater security in the future. This is discussed later.

5. There have been changes in the economic relationship between men and women. In this society there is an accepted division of labour on the basis of sex similar to that described by Oluwasanmi and Dema (1966) in an agricultural

community where defined roles in farm work are assigned to males and females. This division of labour appears to work well under traditional and static conditions but under conditions of change, especially where one sex receives added earnings from a traditional occupation over and above the earnings of the spouse, the respective roles of husband and wives come under pressure. Such additional earnings are not resented if they are mere windfalls. However a permanent upward shift in earnings, especially if due to exogeneous factors and not to an increase in actual labour input, tends to lead to a greater independence of the spouses. It does not necessarily lead to a raising in the level of household subsistence but has other effects on consumption patterns, discussed later.

Other writers have considered the changing roles of men and women under conditions of economic growth. Martin (1963) writing about Uganda, considers that women are less likely than men to perceive the uses of increased income and considers this might be a constraint to agricultural change. De Wilde (1957, vol. I) attributes the reluctance to adapt specialisation in agricultural production in a way which would maximise income, to a number of factors, one of the more important being 'the duality of the household economy—the lack of full identity of interest among men and women with respect both to production and to the expenditure of income'. Household expenditure patterns in Battor certainly demonstrate that the household cannot be considered as a single unit in which effort and expenditure are directed towards optimising its welfare.

Two characteristics of the household expenditure pattern can be distinguished. First, there is a traditional division between a husband's responsibilities and those of his wives for buying goods for household use. Secondly, because of differences in amount of money involved and in the periodicity of earnings there is a difference in the periodicity of men's or women's expenditure on household goods. Men, because they are seasonal farmers or fishermen, tend to have highly seasonal incomes. Women, because they are traders, food processors, etc., have an income spread more evenly throughout the year. Though clam fishing has been a highly seasonal employment, many women find other work, for example, in trade, at other times of the year.

Before an explanation can be given of the level of expenditure on durable household goods, the social institutions which determine family expenditure must be understood. A cultural constraint operates in the division of domestic responsibility between husband and wives. Though both may have the same ultimate aspirations, the traditional division of responsibility for purchasing household needs requires women to provide food, household utensils and clothing needs of children while husbands provide certain domestic durables and producer goods. Though, in a static economy, the latter are probably minor, they now include mosquito nets, furniture, bedding and building materials and a seasonal gift of cloth to the wife. There is of course some flexibility from one family to another in this pattern.

It appears that in a society undergoing economic change in which a wider range of new and attractive goods is presented to the consumer, the division of responsibility for household expenditure become less definitely apportioned between spouses especially if their incomes increase. By 1964 it was still possible in this community to differentiate between purchases made by wives and husbands. Women continued to buy household goods but their purchases covered a much wider range than in 1954, including for example imported domestic durables, plastic dishes, household linen, etc. The significant characteristic of this type of expenditure however is that each item is inexpensive, it does not require very much additional effort to acquire, it is within a woman's means if she wants it sufficiently, and thus it could be effectively effort-inducing. Women's work in this area, and probably for much of Ghana, is of a kind which earns small but quick returns. Here women dive for clams which they sell immediately, or trade for cash, or they process fish or cassava for sale. This is in complete contrast to much of men's income, much of which is concentrated around harvest time, or around the main fishing season. During these periods the man makes most of his customary expenditures many of which are heavy, and also those expenses of a semi-capital nature, e.g. repayment of past debts, cost of litigation, purchase of furniture and housebuilding materials, education fees.

The surplus remaining after these expenses may be saved. In earlier periods, however, the seasons for harvest and fishing, which provided the main sources of income, were associated with festivals and ceremonies at which large expenditures were involved, especially in providing drink, which frequently left the farmers and fishermen with little spare cash. These festivals have decreased in prominence since 1954 and the farmer has greater alternative uses for his cash. The 'lumpiness' of men's income provides a potential source of savings. This study also revealed that considerable savings had accumulated in the past, usually unknown to relatives and often hoarded in some unobservable form, e.g. in cash hoards or in investment in cattle, which is also considered as a hoard.

6. There has been a considerable increase in casual and part time work which has yielded an increase in transitory income and this in turn has affected saving and expenditure.

Another feature of the economy in transition which affects savings and consumption habits is the difference between permanent and transitory income streams. Observations here support Friedman's theory of consumer behaviour that the 'permanent' average propensity to consume is independent of the level of 'permanent' income, but depends on other variables (Friedman, 1957).

Income streams in this society fall into three categories:

(a) Permanent income from traditional sources yielding a steady average income.
(b) Transitory income from traditional sources which yields an occasional windfall (e.g. exceptional harvest, sudden rise in prices due to exogeneous factors, such as imposition of import duties on food).
(c) Transitory income from other employment, e.g. casual wage employment.

An increase in permanent income streams occurred between 1954–64 largely due to the increased land brought under cultivation and improved prices for local foodstuffs. Friedman recognises that it takes time for an individual to adjust his consumer habits to a higher level of permanent income. In a traditional farming community the length of this time lag is prolonged by constraints to consumption discussed later, and partly by the uncertainty of harvests, weather and prices which, in a generally non-diversified agriculture, make farm incomes highly variable from year to year. Thus when crop prices rise and farm incomes rise it is difficult for farmers to know whether this represents an increase in transitory income or an increase in permanent income. This uncertainty has the effect of restraining an immediate increase in the permanent level of consumption. This allows savings to accumulate. Savings are thus not only related to transitory incomes but to rises in income which are seen *ex post facto* to be permanent. The greater the uncertainty and insecurity of the future, the greater these savings are likely to be and the slower the consumer will respond to increased permanent income streams by raising his level of consumption.

In 1954 permanent income from traditional sources was spent on maintaining the culturally determined level of consumption. This level included expenditure on festivities and ceremonies. However as incomes from traditional sources rose between 1954–64, the culturally determined level of subsistence did not rise proportionately and this enabled a rising proportion of savings to be made out of permanent income. Transitory income from traditional sources was formerly spent on exceptionally large festivities and ceremonies. In 1964–67 however, most was spent on prestige housing. Transitory income from casual employment tends to be spent on consumer durables which do not immediately enter into the culturally determined level of consumption, e.g. bicycles, transistor radios, and gambling. Any income, however, which can be concealed from the family may be saved secretly. It is usually impossible to conceal permanent income obtained from traditional sources and any savings made from this are generally known to the family. The main sources of secret hoards are provided by transitory incomes.

The most striking economic phenomenon in this community between 1954–64 was the volume of savings which were made secretly. Before these can be discussed in more detail however, it is necessary to examine other motivations and constraints which existed.

ii. *Motivations and Constraints to Change*

In his model of limited aspirations, Mellor (1964) considers growth to be a function of the changing aspirations of the farmer in which his preference for leisure is changed to a preference for material goods and services. Many low income societies, it is said, conform to a low level of aspirations. Once subsistence needs have been met the marginal utility of additional goods and services falls very rapidly and there is a high utility of leisure.

The main assumptions of Mellor's limited aspirations model are that the marginal utility of additional income drops substantially once subsistence is met and the productivity of labour is such that incomes commonly range around the subsistence level.

To test Mellor's hypothesis against the evidence of this empirical study, the aspirations for which this society is striving will be considered first, and secondly, a more careful examination will be made of what a number of writers easily dismiss as 'leisure' in a rural society and this will be related to the marginal productivity of labour.

(a) LIMITED ASPIRATIONS

In the Lower Volta, cultural factors have, in the past, placed a limit on aspirations for material goods and services. Mellor has considered aspirations to be expressed in the present demand for material goods and services. This, however, appears to be a very superficial approach to understanding the aspirations of traditional society. Much more careful study is needed to determine the motivations, the means and ends, of individuals at this stage of growth. Many aspirations exist which cannot be exhibited in the form of material goods, at least not immediately, and these may provide a motivation for savings and not consumption. The individual is involved in the choice between present or future goods and, under conditions of great insecurity, it is probable that, to the individual, after a certain level of consumption has been satisfied, future goods may be worth more than present goods.

The need to conserve funds for the future may involve the individual in concealing his resources from the voracious demands of his immediate and extended family. Societies in which there are cultural constraints to growth in the level of consumption, have, under condition of economic development and rising incomes, increased funds for savings. An illustration of this is given by Field (1960, p. 32) who wrote of the tremendous difference between an individual's level of income and consumption in Ghana. 'An industrious cocoa farmer may make up to thousands of pounds a year but seldom is any of this spent on raising the basic standard of living'.

Aspirations can cover three types of good, first present material goods and services, including those items entering into the standard of living including consumer durables and producer goods; secondly future goods and services, and thirdly, leisure. Standards of living in the present will be considered first.

In the Lower Volta strong constraints on the level of consumption were found. It is not the purpose here to attempt to explain, at a socio-cultural level, why these constraints should operate but they are considered to be fairly typical of many traditional societies. Sanctions which enforce these constraints have been discussed elsewhere. Foster for example discusses the ways in which a community expresses its distaste for any inbalance in its structure (Foster, G. M., 1965), and most of these are commonplace in the Lower Volta. 'Two rules give guidance to preferred behaviour: do not reveal evidence of material or other improvement in your relative position lest you invite sanctions; should you display improvement, take action necessary to nullify it'. 'A family deals with the problem of suspected improvements in its relative positions by, first, attempts to conceal evidence that might lead to this conclusion or second, admits an improvement in his relative position but neutralises it through ritual expenditure.'

The dominating mores which determine consumption habits in this society and which restrain it from moving to a higher level have been discussed in more detail elsewhere (Lawson, 1967b). Basically, consumption patterns are culturally determined. Deviation from the norm is only allowed to those whom Hoselitz (1957) has named 'marginal individuals' and who in this society are represented by the 'strangers' especially the educated elite in salary employment. The traditional fisherman-farmer must conform to an established consumption pattern on threat of public sanction. Foster lists some of the public sanctions which enforce these constraints, and these equally apply to the society studied here—gossip, slander, backbiting, 'character assasination', witchcraft or the threat of witchcraft, sometimes actual physical aggression. Dominating all is the concern with public opinion.

In spite of such constraints the culturally determined subsistence level in the Lower Volta moved to a higher level between 1954 and 1964. Aspirations for material goods had been realised on two levels, by increased expenditure on both consumption goods and consumer durables, as revealed by the household expenditure surveys and inventories of consumer durables, producer goods and animals. Comparisons of 1954 and 1964 levels are given in Table 22. In 1954 nearly 70% of household cash expenditure was used on food and drink (excluding drink at funerals, which took another 2% of the total), and only 2% of this on imported foods. By 1964 expenditure on food had fallen to 55%, though that spent on imported foods had doubled. Of the whole population, nearly all regularly consumed lump sugar, three-quarters used canned milk, one-half used canned fish, and one-quarter used tea, coffee, margarine, tomato puree and canned meat. About the same amount was spent on drink, though by 1964 it has fallen in proportion to total expenditure. Increased items of purchase were medicine, baby foods, clothing, household goods, and education, the latter absorbing 3.5% of total expenditure.

By 1967 the acceptance of certain imported foods into the minimum level had occurred in 50% of the households. Expenditure on clothing had reached a much higher level than previously, largely owing to essential expenditure on children's school uniforms. There is undoubtedly a high income and price elasticity of demand for all imported goods though it was not possible to measure this. An indication of price elasticities occurred in 1965–66 when the price of imported foods rose 40–50% in this area where, in spite of price controls, black market prices ruled. This high price completely halted the replenishment of stocks in stores. Three stores closed down as a result. The only items remaining unsold were items for health and hygiene, some baby food, and a few bottles of soft drinks and these were all old stock.

One could list the various influences which brought about changes in the level of consumption.

(a) The influence of an increasing number of 'strangers'.
(b) New wage employments which brought higher and regular incomes and with it a level of security beyond that accruing to traditional farmer-fisherman.
(c) Greater physical contact with other places, particularly urban areas, largely due to improvements of roads and markets.
(d) New capital investment from exogenous sources e.g. in education and hospitals. These increased the demand for goods connected with school (uniforms, shoes, books, stationery, etc.) convenience foods, and health and hygiene goods.

Some of these influences had a multiplier effect on local employment, particularly those resulting from new investments which created employment for tailors, seamstresses, caterers.

Under static economic conditions such as existed in 1954, not only is expenditure on consumption constrained but expenditure on durables is also constrained. Individuals who own expensive consumer durables or producer goods which have not yet become traditionally acceptable, seek to conceal them. In this area for example, a man who had bought an expensive kente cloth rarely wore it but when he did he said it originally belonged to his father's family. A lorry driver who had in fact amassed considerable wealth and owned a number of lorries, held the lorries in another name and passed himself off as a mere lorry driver.

McClelland considers the ability to display achievement to be a strong driving force giving incentive to growth (McClelland, 1960, Chaps. 6, 7, 8). This society has in fact an established mode of expression of achievement through the construction of prestigous family houses. Beyond this any other display has not been acceptable under static conditions; it would violate the rules and threaten the status of traditional leaders who alone are allowed to demonstrate their wealth ostentatiously though even so, mostly only in a traditional manner. A more flexible display of achievement probably belongs to a society at a more advanced stage of development.

The constraints to expenditure on consumer durables which exist in the traditional sector do not however extend to 'strangers' and to the educated elite i.e. those educated away from the village. A third group of persons exempted from traditional consumption patterns, even if they are natives, are those who have earned income from non-traditional sources—especially if they have been educated away from the village. Persons falling into this category have already moved outside the traditional culture.

In considering aspirations however it is necessary to go beyond a mere comparison of changes in levels of consumption and ownership of domestic durables and producer goods. It is necessary also to compare levels of consumption and incomes. Growth in incomes over 1954–64 greatly outstripped growth in consumption even though consumption levels rose. It might be tempting to consider this as example of the limited aspirations model. This however would be a wrong analysis of the situation, since it assumes that developing economies are highly consumption orientated. The study of the economy of the Lower Volta does not support this contention, where it has been shown that a high propensity to consume is certainly not a phenomenon of rural economic growth though it may be a feature of urban life.

Certain writers consider that the process of transforming leisure into effort in traditional rural economies where there are supplies of under-employed labour, could be hastened by wooing the peasant with the goodies of a western shop window. Mellor (1964) for example, has advocated amongst others, that the incentive to consume should be increased. Deusenberry (1949) depicts consumption drives which induce a high propensity to consume. Yudelman finds that income goals are clearly related to the length of time individuals have been exposed to a Western consumption level and that such exposure encourages the individual to work harder so as to become more sophisticated in his consumer demands (Yudelman, 1964).

While these arguments might apply in certain communities they certainly do not apply to the rural economy studied here at its existing stage of growth, though it is not possible to say whether it might apply at a more advanced level. Ostentatious expenditure is generally disliked and despised in rural Ghana and there are probably fundamental sociological reasons why the society should conform to a traditional pattern of consumption associated with the maintenance of established norms. In 1954 it was found that the dominant consideration of rural people in spending their incomes was to conform to accepted standards of behaviour. Deviation from this brought unpleasant social comment and suspicion. This, however is no justification for assuming that aspirations are limited; aspirations are simply expressed in other ways.

(b) THE SEARCH FOR SECURITY

In a traditional society there are more subtle aspirations which are not directly expressed in effective demand for immediate consumption goods. The most urgent aspiration is for future security and this becomes stronger as economic change threatens the stability of traditional life. The need for security in conditions of change has been discussed by numerous writers but rarely in relation to its economic effect. De Wilde (1967) mentions briefly that 'for many Africans security is a more important consideration than the possibility of increasing income'.

Traditional society has its own built-in system of social security which is provided by the extended family and by the assumption that each household will provide itself with subsistence food needs. At a village level the processes of economic development erode this social security. The extended family breaks up into dispersed nuclear families; those with education leave the village for employment elsewhere; the growth of the cash economy involves the peasant in a reliance on the market; tempting opportunities for casual wage employment attract family labour away from traditional employment. Under such conditions new forms of social insurance must be found for security against old age, sickness, failure of harvests. Linked with fear of insecurity in the future however is the continued desire for good health, fecundity in women, virility in men.

The search for security leads the individual to explore new avenues. Those considered here are religion, education of children, gambling, and the accumulation of secret hoards. First, fear of future or imagined illness involves visits to the fetish and local herbalist. Payments made for protection against demons and future illnesses can be considered as insurance payments for social benefits. Increased recourse to fetish under conditions of economic change was noted in Ghana by Field (1960, p. 29) and Christensen (1959, p. 278). Similar occurrences were observed in the Lower Volta. In 1954, 42 households had their own private fetish shrines, twelve different clan shrines were also identified and all were in constant use. In 1964 the influence of the fetish was stronger though less obviously apparent. Though the village had been exposed to Christian religion in a much more vigorous way than in 1954 and though there were many regular attenders at the Roman Catholic Church, the shrines continued to play a dominant part in the village, even among church members. Christensen, writing about the Fante in Ghana, associated the many new cults and increased consultation at shrines as reflecting an attempt to ameliorate the insecurities prevalent in a society in transition. Both Christensen and Field, writing about the Akan, describe the great increase in the number of new shrines in conditions of insecurity and change. Field talks of 'new shrines seething with vitality whereas all the ancient supernatural sanctions are moribund'.

A second form of security is sought in investment in education of the young on the anticipation that an educated child will earn a higher income and thus be able to assist his parents and family more readily later on and that one well-educated child will give much more financial support than a number of uneducated or partly educated children. Families in Battor tended to invest funds in the education of one child and not to spread their resources thinly over a number of children. The dependence of parents on earnings of children has been noted by Caldwell (1965). In a study of 800 persons in Ghana over the age of 60, Caldwell found that only 5.5% of the retired males and 2.4% of retired females were unable to get financial assistance from children. In an earlier paper Caldwell (1965) found that five-sixths of the students at the University of Ghana expected to disburse on average, about one fifth of their net incomes to between four and six relatives. Foster explaining the value placed on education in Ghana says that the absence of alternative mechanisms for mobility has placed a great premium on the possession of formal educational qualifications (Foster, P. M., 1965).

Investment in education can be considered a rational use of funds and an investment for the future. A similar observation was made in Nigeria where Delane Welsch (1965) reporting on the investment preferences of Abakaliki rice farmers in education states, 'The economic implications of such behaviour are obvious; farmers expect a much higher rate of return on investment in schooling than on investment in fertilisers'. Whilst among the Abakaliki, the rate of return was given as the motivator for investment, in the Lower Volta the investment criteria was security. However, investment in education of children was far more likely to yield a good return than investment in agriculture. In fact investment opportunities in agriculture which were open to peasant farmers in the Lower Volta were negligible, considering the constraints of labour, land and farm management.

In Battor money spent on education greatly increased over the 10-year period. In 1954 it was almost non-existent. By 1964, 2.5% of aggregate income (£400) was spent on education of children in the village and a further 1% (£150) was spent on education undertaken elsewhere. Costs of education include costs of books, uniforms, fees, and subsistence for those away from home.

In an attempt to find the return received by families from educated children a study was made of all the remittances received in, and sent out of Battor over a period of 19 months in 1965–6. Remittances received from relatives living away totalled about £9 per household per annum. However, it was not possible to get sufficient data to correlate remittance receipts with payments made earlier for the education of children but some positive relationship appears to exist between these two.

Another manifestation of the search for security is the increasing attraction of gambling. Gambling did not exist in 1954, but was well established by 1964, mostly in State lotteries. However, during 1964 the village became involved in another form of gambling, a chain letter scheme called 'Sosu' which led to remittance payments of some £180 out of the village. Only £30 was received in return, and after six months, the scheme was exposed as fraudulent and discontinued. Sums spent on State lotteries in 1964 averaged £10 per month. Spread over the population this may seem negligible, but in fact there were only a few persons who habitually spent money in this way and it was largely an outlet for income earned from casual wage employment, i.e. transitory incomes.

Another effect of the search for security is the continued insistence of households on producing enough food to satisfy its subsistence needs at the expense of refusing wage employment. This has been discussed by many writers and was observed also in the resettlement towns of the Volta Lake (Lawson, 1968b). In the Lower Volta it was not uncommon to find men in wage employment taking time off during the planting season to undertake farm work. The effects of maintaining an extensive subsistence sector cannot be discussed in detail here except to comment that it delays the change-over to a full cash economy and thus constrains agricultural growth.

The most important economic effect of the search for security however is the desire to accumulate secret hoards and investments. It has already been considered that investment in cattle is a function of this search for security, and the advantages of cattle owing for this purpose have been discussed. The reasons for secrecy in hoarding or in capital accumulation are not difficult to find. Foster has viewed capital accumulation as a threat to the stability of the traditional community and for this reason it must be done secretly (Foster, G. M., 1965). Another reason is the fear of having wealth taken away by sorcery. Field (1960, p. 122), in commenting on the number of persons who visit shrines, gives one reason for this, 'The great majority are healthy people supplicating for "protection". Financially successful men are full of fear lest envious kinsmen should, by means of bad magic or witchcraft, bring about their ruin'.

Between 1954–64, savings of individuals in the Lower Volta began to accumulate more rapidly. As these were held mostly secretly as cash hoards or in concealed investment in cattle it was not surprising that few people admitted to the accumulation of wealth. However the withdrawal of hoards in 1966–67 for expenditure on prestige housing exposed a level of savings which could only have been accumulated over a period.

Expenditure on housing can be considered in many ways, for example as an investment capable of both yielding income and capital growth or as an increase in the standard of living and level of consumption. In this society, as in much of Ghana's rural economy, it is not mainly any of these. Spending on prestige housing is a traditional display of effort and achievement. Rural housing is not an investment. It has no rental value, such houses often remain unoccupied or only partly occupied. Motivations are not directly economic. They are part of the individual's assurance of status and thus can be considered as another manifestation of his need to establish security in his own society. The Lower Volta, like many other rural areas of Ghana, is scattered with expensive prestige housing which is often unoccupied, unleased, and, when it is occupied, is rarely accompanied with a commensurate level of consumption and durable consumer goods.

The process of heavy expenditure on housing throughout the Lower Volta was triggered off in 1966 by the return of fishermen with large cash incomes from the suddenly prolific fisheries of the new Lake. Their high earnings were not treated by them initially as an increase in permanent income but as transitory incomes. Under static conditions these would be absorbed mostly with expenditure on festivities and on improvements and additions to family houses.

The size of the 'windfall' and the fact that it was common knowledge and could not therefore be concealed, induced fishermen to spend their earnings on more lavish housing. This spending however had an immediate effect on others who had been able to accumulate secret savings from other sources over the years and there was a sudden withdrawal of savings by those, including women, who had not been fishing on the Lake, for expenditure on housing. The motivations for this was expressed by a farmer who had not been fishing and who was determined to demonstrate his achievement, made over the years, who said he was going to start to build his house before he went to the Lake just to show people that he had earned his money by hard work and not by luck! The withdrawal of investments in cattle by certain individuals in Battor and in other villages in this riparian area was observed during 1966–67. Some persons who were confronted with suddenly having funds which, it was known had not been earned from fishing, admitted to having built up secret hoards elsewhere.

While investment in cattle has been shown to be good business, hoarded cash resources represent an economic loss to the community. Investment in prestigious housing probably also represents economic loss, though it may be a necessary step to a more profitable use of surplus funds later on. The mobilisation of rural savings in a way which satisfies all the demands of the farmer, is one of the challenges facing governments of developing countries.

iii. *The Marginal Productivity of Labour and the Use of Leisure*

A study of motivations would be incomplete without knowing more about the farmers use of time. Many studies of tropical agriculture have shown a very low level of labour input into farm work. The description of marginal productivity of such labour as zero or near to zero is commonplace in the literature. Though the concept of the backward bending supply curve is now treated as an exception and not a rule, many writers emphasise the high premium placed on leisure. However, a number of criticisms can be made against using labour-input to measure productivity of farm labour. As pointed out by Karcz (1968) and others, labour input is not of a constant quality, it varies in energy value during the day, over the season and from farmer to farmer. Such variability occurs in most occupations, in wage employment as well as self-employment. Time paid for by an employer includes a certain amount of unproductive time. No allowance is made for this when measuring labour input into agriculture in terms of hours worked and thus the labour productivity figures tend to be biased upwards. However the neglect to measure the value of other uses of time, some of which will be discussed, biases labour productivity estimates downwards.

It is the contention here that concepts of leisure and marginal productivity of labour in traditional societies cannot be understood without examining the full use of farmers' time. It is not difficult to measure the productivity of labour used in wage employment and which produces a good of measurable value. However, in traditional agriculture, much time may be spent on activities which do not earn a direct or indirect cash income but which nevertheless are of some economic value. Much more attention has recently been focussed on the value and labour cost of those activities in traditional societies which are not usually considered to be economically productive (Jones, 1968). These include first, time spent on ceremonies, religious and entertainment services, etc., and other activities which help to maintain the cultural framework of traditional society, and secondly, other activities which do in fact have a visible productive value, e.g. the provision of housing, clothing, and road maintenance, domestic crafts, manufacture and maintenance of producer goods and others, for household consumption. Though all these are classified in the literature as Z goods (non-farm goods) they can in fact be differentiated. We could consider the first set of goods (ceremonies, services, etc.) as Z^1 and the second as Z^2.

In the literature it is generally assumed that in a rural society the production of Z goods (non-agricultural goods) and F goods (agricultural goods) make competing demands on the time of the farmer. Hymer and Resnick (1969) have constructed a model based on Ghana in which there is high degree of mobility between the production of Z and F goods and in which the production of Z and F goods form competing uses for the farmer's time. The possibility of choice between producing Z or F goods is basic to their model. However, in much of Ghana, this assumption is completely invalid. The production of both Z^1 and Z^2 goods is, as already indicated, carried on in the Lower Volta during the off-crop season and at times when there is no fishing. The use of time on Z^1 goods, e.g. ceremonies, (but not funerals) is associated with harvest and take place after the peak period of labour input. Other festivities are associated with the return of fishermen at the end of the fishing season. More time spent on F may require more time to be spent on certain Z^1 goods, for example, a more successful and bountiful harvest or fishing season frequently gives rise, in the static traditional society, to a longer and more costly festive season.

Employment on Z^2 goods such as communal labour, housebuilding, the repair and maintenance of nets, basket making and others are also undertaken in the off-season and do not form competing uses for the farmer's productive on-farm time. Some of these are in fact complementary goods as, for instance, the preparation of producer goods such as trap and implement making. More time spent on cultivating a larger area may earn more money which can be spent on improving property on which the farmer may use his own labour. Both house-building and trap and implement making have economic values which could be measured in terms of productivity per hour. However one cannot compare the marginal productivity of labour engaged in direct farm work with that engaged in producing Z^2 goods since they are not competing alternative uses for the farmer's time but are complementary uses and whether there is mobility between them is irrelevant.

Another assumption made by Hymer and Resnick which is not borne out by this empirical study is that there is a high propensity to consume. On the basis of this assumption they have argued that a prerequisite to increased agricultural activity is to reduce the time spent on producing Z^2 by providing the rural economy with manufactured incentive goods, raw materials and capital goods. However, under conditions of high seasonality of labour input, in which the production of Z^2 goods does not make competing demands on time spent on the farm, continued production of Z^2 goods increases the marginal productivity of labour at a period when otherwise it might be near to zero. It has already been shown that traditional rural societies are not easily wooed by the glamour of a western shop window and that change in the level of consumption is very sluggish at this level of the economy. In economic decision making the need for security takes precedence over the desire to increase the level of consumption.

Apart from the production of Z^1 and Z^2 goods discussed above, there are other labour activities which cannot be measured either in labour time input or in immediate economic value and yet are of essential value for future material needs. For example, there is the need to retain good relations with the extended family, with the clan and village. These are a necessary part of the social security of traditional life. They also involve the expenditure of time and effort. Relatives must be visited, family and clan affairs must be attended to. These activities are part of the payment for social security benefits expected in the future and can be labelled as Z^3 goods. Though these may have a long term pay-off they form an essential part of the traditional way of life.

In the sample of farmers studied at Battor and discussed earlier, an average of 139 days per farmer were mainly spent on travelling, visiting the market, funerals, ceremonies and resting, compared to days 205 spent on economic activities. The labour input into economic activities which yield immediate visible and measurable returns (F and Z^2 goods) cannot be considered in isolation from labour input into socio-economic activities which yield benefits in the future (Z^1 and Z^3 goods), which are difficult to quantify, since the decision to spend time on the former is partly determined by the projected marginal utility of time spent on the latter.

Traditional agriculture is a way of life and one cannot consider farm work in isolation from other uses of farmers' time. The concept of value in terms of time spent on production has meaning only when one considers the total use of time, including what is euphemistically called leisure, measured against the total value of goods and services produced in traditional society. The traditional farmer uses his time not only to produce goods which have an immediate exchange price but also to render those services which may have a future pay-off for him, for example in social benefits.

In order to measure the value of present income to the individual one has to consider what happens to his immediate cash earnings. It is common to consider that the dissipation of earnings amongst the extended family brings little or no net return to the individual. However if a redistribution of earnings over the extended family secures his status in the village and produces the anticipation of greater security in the future, the individual may feel this is sufficient incentive to effort. However he may also feel that security and status could equally well be obtained not by cash hand-outs but by cementing his relationship with the extended family, as for example, by more frequent visiting and greater attention to family affairs. This type of activity is commonly labelled 'leisure'. It is a mistake however, to consider that this sort of activity has no actual or anticipated economic return.

The preservation of rural institutions involves the individual in expenditure of time and effort. In allocating his time between different uses, the individual is in fact not only measuring marginal productivities of different alternative employments but also measuring them against the marginal productivity of time spent on those traditional activities which give him status and security in his society. These, together, probably make the real opportunity cost of labour in traditional societies much higher than is usually estimated. It should not be surprising therefore to find a sluggish supply response from farmers to increases in prices of traditional crops. He has other alternative uses for his time.

Many studies in developing economies have shown a high positive response to price, though this has usually been demonstrated in societies beyond the stage of growth discussed here. The farmers described here cannot be compared for instance, to Dean's Malawi tobacco farmers (Dean, 1966) since they had passed beyond the transitional stage and could migrate to take wage employment as an alternative to tobacco growing. Neither can they be compared with cocoa farmers in Ghana described by Hill (1963) since cocoa farming represented a new frontier which released the farmer from his traditional farming existence and enabled him to invest in a speculative enterprise usually some distance from his home village, in a manner not unlike investment in cattle today in the Lower Volta.

To the farmer, the weighing up of the opportunity cost of leisure is probaby much more subtle and more dominated by economic motivations than hitherto considered. The individual is not just simply weighing the utility of leisure against the disutility of work, as Mellor conceived it (Mellor, 1964); he is weighing the utility of more income against the disutility of having to expose earnings, and the utility, for the future, of concealed savings.

iv. *Conclusion*

To consider time spent visiting relatives, or at the markets, or even just sitting around in the village, as leisure, is to misunderstand the economic choice available in traditional rural economies. The concept of rural leisure in such societies has been seriously misunderstood largely because of a failure to understand the villager's involvement with his future needs and his dependence on social security as provided by existing social institutions. His concern with social security increases as society undergoes economic change. It is likely that, under these conditions, any additional time and funds available will be spent first in securing the future before increasing the level of consumption.

Many writers stress the hurdle of getting past the level of subsistence production but, given the right opportunities to increase earnings, it is possibe that this hurdle is overcome not by the incentive to spend but the incentive to save for the future. At this stage of growth, secret hoards or investments may represent the best way of saving income which is surplus to the culturally determined subsistence standards. In the Lower Volta, in spite of increases in income, the continued low standard of living was not an indication of the limited level of aspirations, but, first, of the fear to display property and income publicly (except for the acceptable display of prestige housing), second, of the need to build up security through hoarding, and third, of the socio-cultural constraints on spending on consumption. At this transitional stage of growth, society is not consumption-oriented but security-oriented.

It appears that an essential part of the economic growth process in rural Ghana is the display of status and achievement by prestige expenditure on housing. This display may be delayed, even though funds are available, by an individual's desire not to be conspicuous or deviate from others in his society. Expenditure on housing does not usually represent investment in a marketable asset, except in towns where there is a demand for housing from wage earners. Neither does expenditure on housing involve the individual in raising his level of consumption of household durables since these do not change and the traditional way of life continues. Having displayed achievement in prestigious house building, the individual is still faced with the need to save against insecurity of the future. As long as he remains in a traditional society he is able to do this because there continues to be a social constraint on spending on certain types of consumer goods.

Economic growth which has occurred in the Lower Volta since 1954 has been almost entirely due to exogeneous forces, particularly government investment in infrastructure and markets and also to new government employments in social services, especially schools, hospitals and local government. These have generated new wage employments and a small multiplier effect has resulted. Increase in demand for food and improved marketing facilities led to a considerable growth in agricultural output, partly at the expense of a withdrawal, up to 1964, from fish production. Though there has probably been no great change in per capita productivity in agriculture, the numbers of adults engaged in food production have increased. The growth of the economy has undoubtedly been constrained by the socio-cultural millieu. Savings accumulated in this area have not been invested in productive investment in a way which would promote self-generating economic growth. The economy is thus still at a transitionary stage but the socio-economic framework has probably become sufficiently flexible to encompass new technical inputs if and when they become available.

It is unlikely that Ghana will solve the problems of agricultural change and rural economic growth until much more is known about the savings, consumption and investment habits of rural people. This study has attempted to throw some light on these economic variables. It has been shown that, contrary to generalised opinion, rural people are not consumption orientated but, in the search for security against the uncertainty of change, they are more concerned with saving. However, not all this saving is directed into productive investment since the conditions required for such investment by rural people are difficult to meet, and it is probable that a great deal of cash hoarding takes place.

Though there has been no structural change in the rural economy, this study has proved that low incomes do not necessarily mean low savings and that, given the prerequisite of security and secrecy there is no reason why low incomes should lead to a low rate of investment. The methods of mobilising these savings and diverting them into investment opportunities, whilst at the same time keeping the propensity to consume down, is one of the major problems of agricultural change and rural economic growth.

Bibliography

Agricultural Census of Ghana. Agricultural Census Office, Central Bureau of Statistics, Accra.

Baldwin, K. D. S. 1957. *The Niger Agricultural Project*. Oxford: Blackwell.

Beckett, W. H. 1947. *Akokoaso*. London School of Economics: Monographs in Social Anthropology, No. 10. London: Lund, Humphries.

Caldwell, J. C. 1965. Extended family obligations and education. *Population Studies*, Vol. XIX. 2.

Christensen, J. B. 1959. The adaptive functions of Fanti priesthood. In *Continuity and Change in African Culture*, W. Bascom and M. J. Herskovits. University of Chicago Press.

Dean, E. R. 1966. *The Supply Responses of African Farmers*. Amsterdam: North Holland Publishing Co.

De Wilde, J. C. 1967. *Experiences with Agricultural Development in Tropical Africa*. (I.B.R.D.) Baltimore: Johns Hopkins Press; London: Oxford University Press. 2 vols.

Duesenberry, J. S. 1949. *Income, Saving and the Theory of Consumer Behaviour*. Harvard.

F.A.O. 1963. Production from Grassland in Ghana. Report 1627. Rome.

Field, M.J. 1960. *Search for Security*. London: Faber.

Foster, G. M. 1965. Peasant society and the image of limited good. *Amer. Anthrop.*, Vol. 67, 2.

Foster, P. M. 1965. *Education and Social Change in Ghana*. London: Routledge and Kegan Paul.

Friedman, M. 1957. *A Theory of the Consumption Function*. Princeton University Press.

Galletti, R., Baldwin, K. D. S., and Dina, I. O. 1956. *Nigerian Cocoa Farmers*. London: Oxford University Press for the Nigeria Cocoa Marketing Board.

Golding, P. T. F. 1962. An enquiry into household expenditure and consumption and sale of household produce in Ghana. *Econ. Bull. of Ghana*. Vol. VI, 4.

Government Statistician, Accra, 1954. Survey of Akuse, Amedica and Kpong.

Grove, D. and Huszar L. 1964. *The Towns of Ghana*. Accra: Ghana Universities Press.

Haswell, R. 1953. *Economics of Agriculture in a Savannah Village*. Colonial Research Studies. No. 8.

Hill, Polly, 1963. *Migrant Cocoa Farmers of Southern Ghana*. Cambridge.

Hoselitz, B. F. 1957. Non-economic factors in economic development. *Amer. Econ. Rev. Proc.*, 47.

Hymer, S. and Resnick S. 1967. A model of an agrarian economy. *Amer. Econ. Rev.* Vol. LIX, 4, 1.

Jones, W. O. 1968. Labour and leisure in traditional African societies. *Social Sciences Research Council*, Vol. XXII, 1.

Karcz, J. F. 1968. Comment on 'Peasant consumption, saving and investment in Mainland China' by J. L. Lau. University of California, Santa Barbara.

Lawson, Rowena M. 1957. The nutritional status of a rural community on the Lower Volta, Gold Coast. *J. W. Afr. Sci. Assn.* Vol III, 1. pp 123–9.

1958. The structure, migration and resettlement of Ewe fishing units. *African Studies*. Vol. XVII, 1.

1963a. The development of the Lower Volta. *Econ. Bull. of Ghana*. Vol. VII, 4.

1963b. The Economic organisation of the *Egeria* fishing industry on the River Volta. *Proc. Malac. Soc. Lond.* Vol. XXXV, Part 6, pp. 273–87.

1967a. Summary of a study of labour input into traditional agriculture on the Lower Volta of Ghana. *J. Ag. Econ.* Vol. XVIII, 3, pp. 403–405.

1967b. Changes in food consumption in a rural community on the Lower Volta, 1954–64. *Nig. J. Econ. and Soc. St.* Vol. IX, 1.

1967c. Innovation and growth in traditional agriculture of the Lower Volta, Ghana. *J. Dev. Stud.* Vol. IV, 1. pp. 138–149.

1968a. Traditional utilisation of labour on the Lower Volta. *Economic Bulletin of Ghana*. Vol. XII, 1. pp. 54–61.

1968b. An interim economic appraisal of the Volta Resettlement Scheme. *Nig. J. Econ. Soc. Stud.* Vol. X, 1.

1970. The evolution of markets and places of centrality in rural areas in southern Ghana. *African Urban Notes*, Vol. V, No. 2, Part 2.

1971. The supply response of retail trading services to urban population growth in Ghana. In *The Development of Indigenous Trade and Markets in West Africa*, ed. C. Meillassoux. London: Oxford University Press for International African Institute.

Martin, A. 1963. *The Marketing of Minor Crops in Uganda*. London: H.M.S.O.

McClelland, D. C. 1960. *The Achieving Society*. Princeton, N. J.: Van Nostrand.

Mellor, J. W. 1964. The use and productivity of farm family labour in early stages of agricultural development. *J. Farm Econ.* XLV, 3, pp. 517–34.

Miracle, M. 1962. African markets and trade in the Copperbelt. In *Markets in Africa*, ed. P. Bohannan and G. Dalton. Evanston, Ill.: Northwestern University Press.

Oluwasanmi, H. A. and Dema, J. S. 1966. *Uboma. A Socio-economic Survey of a Rural Community in Eastern Nigeria*. Bude, Cornwall: Geographical Publications Ltd.

Petr, T. 1967. Fish population changes in the Volta Lake over the period January 1965 to September 1966. *Hydrobiologia*, 30.

Pople, W. and Rogoyska, M. 1969. The effect of the Volta River hydroelectric project on the salinity of the Lower Volta River. *Ghana J. Sci.* Vol. IX.

Population Census of Ghana, 1960. Accra: Census Office.

Purchon, R. D. 1963. A note on the biology of *Egeria radiata*. *Proc. Malac. Soc. Lond.* Vol. XXXV, pp. 251–71.

Reports of the Government Fisheries Department, Accra, for the years 1948 to 1952.

Report of the Government Fisheries Department, Accra, 1951–2.

Schultz, T. W. 1964. *Transforming Traditional Agriculture*. New Haven and London: Yale University Press.

Volta River Project. 1956. Report of the Preparatory Commission. London: H.M.S.O.

Volta River Project. Appendices to the Report.

Walters, Dorothy. 1962. *Report on the National Accounts of Ghana, 1955–61*. Accra: Central Bureau of Statistics.

Welsch, Delane. 1965. Response to economic incentive by Abakaliki rice farmers. *J. Farm Econ.*, Vol. XLVII, 4.

White, H. P. 1954. Environment and land utilisation on the Accra Plains. *J. W. Afr. Sci. Assn.* Vol. I.

Index

Accounting system, used for Battor, 7
Accra, 14, 62; cattle on Plains of, 58; traders from, 27; visits from Battor, 92
achievement, expression of, 102–3; *see also* prestige spending
Ada, 62; cattle owners, 57; communications, 13; market, 62; sources of income, 9
Adidome, 14, 19; fishing, 48; hospital, 20; market, 27, 66, 70–1, 72; population increase, 20; stores, 14, 20; transport businesses, 20; urban characteristics, 20; weaving, 25
Afram, river, 45; aggregate income, *see* income
Agricultural Census of Ghana, 1964, 35
agriculture, 24, 30, 79, 112; aggregate labour input, 44; employment, 19; goods, 110; growth, 107; improvements, 3; output, 36; production decline, 2–3; stations, 16; tools, 69; village income, 37; and Volta Dam, 3; *see also* crops, farming land
Akosombo, migration to, 23
Akuse, 13, 14; clam industry, 9; market, 10, 13, 52, 62, 66, 69–70; stores, 14
Amedica, 13; communications, 13; survey of, 9
Apediwoe Islands, palm oil plantation, 33
aspirations of rural community, 5, 99
Aveyime, as collecting centre, 14; communications, 13; stores, 14; trade, 63
Aveyime market, 6, 10, 27, 43, 60, 66, 67, *68*; Lower Volta produce, 62; prices, 7; quantitative recording, 6; traders, 7; volume of trade, 7

baby foods, 94, 101
bakers, 71
Bakpa, fishermen, 45
barges, cargo, 61
basket work, 25
Battor, 1, 6, 19, 105; building work, 26; clam fishing, 52, *54*; cultivated land, 35–38; education costs, 106; employment, 22, 23, *24*, 27, 30; fishermen, 45; food crops, 30; imports, 7; income, 3, 6, 7, *81*; livestock, 60; market, 61, 62, 63–4, 71–2; migration from, 23; 'place of centrality', 26; road to, 13; stores, 14, 62, 64; study of, 10, 11; volume of trade, *65*, 65–6
'Battor hamlets', 6, 65
bicycles, *86*, 94
bilharzia, 14
black market, 74, 77
Black Volta, river, 45
bread, 64
building, contractors, 71; materials collection, 26; prestige expenditure on, 60
businesses, connected with a market, *68*, 70, 71
cane sugar plantation, 79
canned foods, 71
canoes, 46, 52, *54*, 62, 63; Battor, *83*; marriage gift, 52, 54; transport, 13
capital accumulation, threat to traditional community, 107
capital costs, fishing, *46*
capital investment, multiplier effect, 102; in stores, 75
capital transactions, 8
cash crops, 39, 43, 80; cassava, 31; groundnuts, 31; sold in towns, 77; sweet potatoes, 31
cash hoards, 5, 8, 108, 116
cash income, 33, 113; agriculture, 30; from clams, 55; lake fisheries, 108; *see also* income
cassava, 15, 25, 30, 32, 33, 61, 63, 71, 72
casual work, 22, 28, 97; manual, 22; wage employment, 97, 104

INDEX

cattle, 10; Battor, *83;* grazing time, *57;* high death rate, 57; inaccessibility of, 58; investment in, 59, 60, 89, 109; kraals, 57, 59; markets, 58; numbers of, 57; ownership, 57, 58, 59, 88; secret purchase, 59; source of ready cash, 59, 60
census findings, 16, 27, 53
Central Bureau of Statistics, 10
ceremonies, 91, 97, 98, 108; end of fishing season, 111; time spent on, 110
charcoal, 71, 72
chief, position of, 4, 93
child labour, 35, 39, 40, 41
children, clothing, 94
Christian religion, 16, 18, 105
Chrysichthys sp., 48
cigarettes, 14, 70
clams, 9, 14, 15, 71, 72, 51, *54;* capital input, 52, *54;* diving by women, 6, 25, 34, *81,* 87, 'farms' industry size, 51, *54;* price, 53, 55, relocation of industry, 56; sale of, 69, 72; yield, 53, *54*
clan, individual's relation with, 112; kinship ties, 15; structure, 93
class structure, rudimentary, 92
clerks, 28
cloth, household expenditure on, 66; imported, 63; traders in imported, 61
clothing, 75, 96, 101, 110; demand for, 94; household expenditure on, 66; manufacture, 66, *68,* 69, 71; trade in, 77
cocoa, production, 13, *24*
complementary uses of time, 111
communications, 13; improvements, 66, 94, 102; 'places of centrality', 19
concrete block houses, *84*
consumer goods, 93; durables, 98, 101, 102; locally produced, 69
consumption, constraints, 98; culturally determined, 100; goods, 101; levels of 12, 93
convenience foods, 67, *68*
Convention Peoples Party, 93
cotton spinning, 25
craftsmen, 69, 71; goods for household consumption, 110; income, *81;* at markets, *68,* 71, 76; records, 8; self-employed, 24; small local, 27
creeks, fishing in, 30, 48, 49; irrigation by flooding, 32; lands, 32, 33
crops, *24;* acreage, 9, *37;* Battor, 6; value, 32–3, 43; *see also* agriculture, groundnuts, maize, sweet potatoes, vegetables
cultivation, intensity of, 38; land under, 97; seasonal variation, 35; *see also* agriculture
cultural factors, constraint, consumption, 100; limit aspirations, 99; Schultzian-type, 1, 91

daily records, various occupations, 7
dam, *see* Volta dam
debts, *see* loans
Department of Agriculture, 10, 11
depopulation, 12, 15, 16, 18, 22
development of rural communities, 2
diet, 7; household, 10; seasonal variations, 15
diminishing return to land, 42, 43
District Commissioners, 93
diversity of employment, 28, 34
division of labour, 55, 96
drink, 65, 70, 97; consumed at funerals, 91; expenditure on, 101; imported, 73; profitable stock, 74; sale of, 14; *see also* gin

earnings, 95; agricultural household, *42, 85;* clams, 53, *54;* clerks, *85;* clothes manufacture, *85;* exposed, 114; fishing, 48 *85;* gin manufacture, *85;* level of, 3; lorries, *85;* manufacturing, *85;* at source, 6; stores, trading, *85;* unskilled labour, *85;* windfall, 108; *see also* income
economic change, 2, 3
economic growth, 24, 91, 95, 104; effects of Volta dam, 3; preconditions for, 2, 93; road improvement, 78; static, 102
education, 26, 79, 101, 102, 105, compulsory, 41; costs of, 97; elite, 103; further, 22; investment in, 105, 106; need for, 27; rural communities, 4; standards of, 22; Tongu District, 14

employment, *see* agriculture, casual work, child labour, clam industry, craftsmen, diversity of employment, farming, fishing, government, labour input, loss of educated persons,

occupation, salaried workers, seasonal employment, shoemakers, teachers, traders, wage employment, women's work
Ewe tribe, 1
exported goods, 25, 31
extended family, 15, 55, 104; provision for, 113; relations with, 112
family, demands, 99; expenditure, 96; houses, 15; labour, 43; *see also* clan, extended family
fancy goods, traders, 61
farming, 27, 28, 31; Battor, 6, *83*; equipment, *83*; income from, *81*, 98; main occupation, 25, 34, *36*; primary industry, 13; sale of produce, 69, 72; subsidiary occupation, 34, *36*; techniques, 31; *see also* agriculture
fetish shrines, 105, 107
field crops, *24*
firewood, sale of, 25
fish, 13, 62; Battor area, 9; catches, 46, 48; exported, 48, 49; fresh and dried, 15; population, 50; sale of, 69, *72*; sea, 62, 71, *72*; seasonal import, 62; subsistence, 48; traders, 61; trap and net manufacture, 25; yields, 9
Fisheries Department, 10, 11, 51
fishing, 22, *24*, 27, 28, 29, 34, 87; Battor, 6, *83;* capital costs, 46, *46;* coastal, 2; earnings, 48; equipment, 25, 69, *83*, 111; income, 2, *46*, 47 *81*; inland, 2, 22–3, 45; loss after dam built, 3; main occupation, 25; primary industry, 13; seasonal employment, 23, 45, 46; tidal, 48; Volta lake, 3, 80, 82
floods, 2, 33, 48, 51, 54, 80; communications difficulty, 13; economic importance, 32,
food, consumption, 7, 43; convenience, 67, *68*; expenditure on, 101; increased demand for, 115; interchange in rural areas, 77; price increase, 43; price of local, *36*, *37*, sale of prepared, 72; *see also* diet, fish, fruit
forest products, exchange in market, 62
Forestry Department, 11
fruit, sale of, 30, 69, *72*
Fulani, herdsmen, 57; meat traders, 61
funerals, 15, 23, 91; Battor, 91
future security, need for, 104

gambling, 107
Ghana, independence, 4, 16
Ghana National Household Expenditure data, 30
gin, 66, 71; consumption, 91; distilling, 25; illicit, 62; local illicit, 73
glass making, 26
gold ornaments, Battor, *83*
goods for sale, Adidome market, *72*; Aveyime market, 66, *67, 68*; Sogakope market, *72*
government, employment, 115; investment, 3, 20–1, 26, 27, 31, 115; road building, 13
gramophones, *86*, 94
Gross Domestic Product, 87
groundnuts, 14, 15, 25, 30, 32, 33, 61, 63, 71, *72*
guns, *83*, *86*
haberdashery, 61, 63, 64
harvest, 33, 39; ceremonies, 111; uncertainty of, 98; women's work, 32
Hausa, herdsmen, 57; meat traders, 61
health, Tongu district, 14
hospitals and clinics, 79, 102; Battor, 72; built by missions, 16–18; rural communities, 4
households, assets, *86*, 88; daily food consumption, 7; durables, 73, *73*, 77, 88, 93, 96; expenditure, 6, 7, 95, 96; goods, 75, *83*, *86*, 94; holding of land, 35, *37*; income, 24–5, *37*, 42, *82*; threat to traditional, 55
house building, 15, 88, 97; Adidome, *85;* Battor, 10, *85*; boom in, 80–1; cost of input, 10; improvements, 3, 5, 89; investment in, *85*; in off-season, 111
housing, 79, 110; Battor value, *83, 84;* boom, 88; differences, 89; prestige, 98
husbandry, 57, 59
husband's expenditure on household goods, 95

illiteracy, *see* literacy, education
implements, cost of, 40
imported food, 73, 76, 101; in Akuse market, 70; expenditure on, 8; stores dependence on, 77; tinned fish, 65
imported goods, 14, 70–1; cloth, 64; drink, 8; in markets, 66, *67, 68*, 70, 71, 75, 76; in stores, 64, toys, 71
income, aggregate village, 27, *37* 86–7;

INDEX

agricultural, 6, *37;* clam diving, 52, *54;* diversity of sources, 27; from fishing, 2, 3, 6, 46, *46,* 49, *49;* growth of per capita, 4; household, 24–5, *37*, 42, *82*; levels of, 12; man's seasonal, 96; permanent, 97, 98; subsidiary sources of, 28, 34; sources in Battor, 6; surplus held as cash hoard, 5; targets of rural communities, 5; *see also* cash income, earnings
inflation, 60, 87, 88
investments, in cattle, 5, 107, 108; in education, 5, 105, 106; need for opportunities, 4, 116
iron goods, 70
irrigation, from annual floods, 2; schemes, 31
itinerant workers, craftsmen, 76; meat traders, 64; women food traders, 67, *68*

kenkey (fermented corn), 64
Keta district, 13, 62
knives, 63
Koforidua, 14, 27
kokonte, *see* cassava

labour costs, agricultural, *36*
labour input, 34, 35, 39; average daily, 40; economic activities, 112; farming, 10, 28, 38, 107; fishing, 49, *50*; household, 43; seasonal, 40, 111; socio-economic activities, 112; variable, 109
labour mobility, 26, 27, 55, 56, 94
labour productivity, 40–1, 86–7, 110
land, marginal, 35, 43; rotating system, 31; under cultivation, 6, 9, 35 *37*; utilization, 42, 43
leisure, 99, 110, 114
level, of aspirations, 114; of consumption, 103; of income, 103
literacy, 12, 14, *see* education
litigation, 12, 96
livestock, *24,* 63; *see* cattle
living expenses, 47
living standards, *see* standard of living
loans, 8, 47, 97
local government offices, 16
local produce, diversity of, 77; drink, 8; expenditure on, 8; foodstuffs, 73; immigrants' demand for, 76; in markets, *67, 68,* 72; price of, 97; sale of, 78

lorries, 62, 66, *67,* 68–9, 102; passenger, 92; transport to Battor, 75
loss of educated persons, 104

maize, 13, 14, 25, 30, 32, 79
malaria, 14
manufacturing, *24;* Battor, 26
marginal land, 35, 43
marginal productivity of labour, 28, 109, 111
marginal propensity to save, 89
market, 43, 44; centre for local produce, 75; centre for small industries, 76; development of, 27, 66, *67, 68,* 71, 72; government investment in, 21; growth, 85, 77, 78, 79; imported goods, 75; improvement, 4, 35, 115; prices, 53; purchase recording, 6; *see also* Ada, Adidome, Akuse, Aveyime, Battor, Sogakope, Tefle
medicines, 27, 64, *73*, 75, 94, 101
Mepe, fishermen, 45; road to, 13
migration, and education, 104; fishermen, 46, 50; permanent, 23; temporary, 15, 23; Tongu, 12, 22; women clam divers, 52
mobility, increased consumption levels, 94
monthly records, store-keeping, 7; trading 7

native soap making, 25
natural capital growth, cattle, 60
nets, traps, 25, 46
Nkrumah regime, 93
non-agricultural employment, 21
non-agricultural goods, 110
non-labour inputs, agriculture, 40, *41*
non-productive functions, 12
nutrition, *see* diet

occupation, changes in Battor, 23, *24;* related to education, 22; structure in Tongu District, 23, *24; see also* employment, labour input
onions, 13, 62, 63
onchocerciasis, 14
Oti, river, 45
output per household, 30
pagan religion, 12, 15; *see also* fetish shrines
palm oil, 15; plantations, 30, 33
palm wine, 66

INDEX

parents' dependence on children's earnings, 105–6
permanent income, 97, 98
physical mobility of labour *see* labour mobility
'places of centrality', 16, 19; administration, 19; composition of population, 21–2; population growth, 19–20
planting season, 39
politics, 4; power of 'chief', 4; structure, 12
population, 1, 21–2; changes, 16, 18, 20; growth, 19–20, 21; places of centrality, 21; *see also* rural population
Population Census, 1960, 14, 18
pottery industry, 25, 71
prestige spending, 104; on cattle, 58; house building, 82, 108, 115; savings for, 90
price, clams, 53; elasticities, 101; local foodstuffs, 36, 37, 76; store goods, 6
primary industry, *see* agriculture, farming, fishing
producer goods, 102; locally made, 69
production, foodstuffs, 43; for the market, 6; sale records, 10; for subsistence, 6
productivity, 37, 115; marginal, 28, 109, 111
profitability, stores, 6, 74
propensity to consume, 103, 116
public opinion, as consumption constraint, 101

quantitative field data, 1

radios, 86, 94
relatives, *see* family, extended family
religion, *see* Christian, pagan
rent, stores, 75
rice, 79; transport of, 13–14
riparian *see* rural
river, blindness, *see* onchocerciasis; transport, 13, 20, 62, 70; *see also* fishing; floods; transport
roads, building in rural communities, 4; government investment, 16, 21; improvement, 20, 35, 63, 79; maintenance, 110; rural improvement, 77–8; traffic, 27; transport, 20 *see also* lorries

Roman Catholic Church, 105
rural economy, choice, 114; economic change, 2, 80; early growth, 2, 115; need for investment, 109; Schultzian-type equilibrium, 1
rural population, consumption, 98, 100, 116; investment, 4, 116; newcomers joining, 4; savings, 109, 116; security orientated, 116; *see also* population
salaried workers, 7, 8, 20, 65, 81, 87; consumption differences, 100–1; in rural community, 4
selling, in Adidome market, 71, 72; to Battor residents, 65; cattle, 58; in the market, 67, 68, 72; to non-residents, 65
salt, 62, 63, 71, 72
sardinella, 63
savings, 87, 94; accumulation, 89; cash, 5, 8, 108, 116; as cattle, 60; difficulty of assessment, 8; for future security, 99, 115; not generating growth, 115; in gold, 9; house-building, 80–1; invested, 8–9; from low incomes, 116; secrecy of, 4, 9, 81, 89, 90, 97, 98, 99, 105, 109, 114; seine net owners, 47; from trade, 89; from transitory income, 98; women's, 89
schools, *see* education
seasonal differences in clam production, 52, 54; employment, 25, 28, 45, 46, 95; fishing, 45, 46; trade at Sogakope market, 71
security, against old age, 104–5; attitudes to, 5; in economic change, 4; provision of future, 113; importance, 5, 112; income, 27; investment in housing, 108; need for, 107; oriented society, 114; savings for, 5, 98, 107; subsistence production for, 107
Sege, communications, 13
seine nets, 46, 48; 'company', 47; earnings, 47; owners, 47, 49
shoemakers, 66, 68, 69, 76
shoes, 70, 94
skilled labour, records, 8
small industries, centred on market, 69, 70–1
social benefits, 113; security importance, 114; services, 19, 27;
socio-cultural changes, 1, 91

INDEX

socio-economic changes, 1, 3—4, 10
Sogakope, 19, 27; market, 10, 44, 66, 71, 72; urban characteristics, 20
sorcery, 107
specialisation, development by traders, 69
specialised crops, 77
spending, cycles, 90; ostentatious, 104; social constraints on, 114, 115
standard of living, 5, 80, 87—8, 89, 100
State, farms, 79; lotteries, 107
statistical recording, of field data, 1
status, display of, 315; housing, 108; symbols, 93
storekeeping, 74 elastic occupation, 77; subsidiary income source, 75
stores, 80, 102; Adidome, 70—1; Akusa market, 70; Battor, 72—3, 74; development of, 69, 71; income from, *81*; Lower Volta, 61; monthly accounts, 6; profits, *65*; purchase recording, 6; stocks, 6, *65*, 74; turnover, *65*
strangers, influence level of consumption, 102; integration into villages, 93; in new employment, 22
subsidiary farming work, 39; occupations, 26; sources of income, 26
subsistence, farming, 25, 26, 28, 45; food needs, 76, 104, 107; level of, 40, 93, 101; production, 24, 34, 43, 49, 52, *54*; 114; sector of economy, 12
sugar, cane farming, 29, cube purchase, 65
sweet potato, 14, 25, 30, 32, 61, 63

teachers, 28, 93—4
Tefle, 13, 19; clam fishing, 51; fishing, 45; intensity of cultivation, 38; market, 13, 44; stores in, 14; survey of river at, 9; wage employment, 27

temporary camps, 52
time, use of, *38*, 112
tobacco, 14, 65, 70, 73
Togoland, migrant labour, 33
Tongu District, 6; fishermen, 12, 45; health, 14; migration from, 22; occupational structure, 23, *24*; road building, 13; schools, 14
Torgome, clam fishing, 51
tractors, 31

trade, Lower Volta, 61; total in Battor, *75*; transit, 14
traders, clam fishery, 53, *54*; collecting, 63; dominant, 55; fancy goods, 61; fish, 61; full-time, 69, 71; itinerant, 69, 92; in markets, 76; part-time, 64; regular daily, 64; women, 61
traditional consumption patterns, 103, 104
traditional society, 95, 90, 112; ceremonies and activities, 23, 113; maintenance of, 110; socio-cultural constraints, 4; leaders, 93, 103
tribal structure, 1, 4, 93
transitory income, 97, 98; spent on gambling, 107
transport, businesses, 20, 71; employment, 27; improvement, 77; related to population, 18, 20; river, 13, 20, 70; road, 13; *see* canoes, roads, lorries
travelling, expenses, 47; to towns, 92; for trade purposes, 92; *see* visiting
turnover, stores, 6, 14, 74

United Africa Company, launch service, 13, 61
United Ghana Farmers' Co-operative Council, 31
University of Ghana, 11, 106
unskilled labour, 8, 28
upland areas, 32
urban institutions, 16
vegetables, 15, 71, *72*; egg plant, 30; okro, 30; peppers, 15; sale of, 69, *72*
village, individual's relations with, 112; large new, 79
visiting, 91—2; family, 113, 114; by farmers, 92; markets, 114; towns, 92
Volta Dam, study, 2, 56
Volta Lake, 22, 34, 45; development of, 23, 80; fisheries, 3, 50, 80, 82
Volta, river, *see* river, fishing, floods, transport
Volta River Authority, 22
Volta River Project Preparatory Commission, 2, 3, 10

wage employment, 7, 16, 20, 21, 24, 27, 31, 79, 94, 115; Battor, 26; influencing consumption, 68, 102; multiplier effect, 27; new, 22; 'places of centrality', 19; attracting strangers, 22; in rural areas, 4, 18; security, 102

weaving industry, 25
wholesale buyers, 66
women, changing role of, 95; domestic responsibilities, 96; evenly spread income, 95; expenditure on household goods, 95; imported clothes, 71
women's work, 43, 45, 52, 53, *54*, 55, 96; clam diving, 6, 25, 51, *54*; farming, 32, 39; pottery, 25; trading, 53, *54*, 64